Seventy-seven keys

keys

to
the civilization
of Japan

© 1985 by Tadao Umesao

ISBN: 0-89346-267-5

Heian International, Inc.
P.O. Box 1013
Union City, California 94587

86 87 88 89 90 10 9 8 7 6 5 4 3 2 1

Printed in Korea

Preface

Not very long ago I visited Paris at the invitation of the French Ministry of Foreign Affairs and gave some lectures on the cultural dimensions to Japanese public planning and related subjects. While I was there I found that I had been given a sobriquet and that I was known as 'the messenger from the black hole'. Why such a sobriquet? Because, the explanation ran, a black hole was exactly what Japan was when viewed from France. While Japan continued to absorb information from all over the world, not the slightest bit of information was to be found leaving Japan. Since I had come from Japan to speak about Japanese culture in France, it was natural that I should be referred to as 'the messenger from the black hole'.

One has to admit that there is some truth to this. Modern Japan may well appear to owe its development to a succession of borrowings: after all, it derived its earliest system of government administration from Chinese civilization; it borrowed from the cultures of Portugal and the Netherlands in the seventeenth and subsequent centuries; it assimilated the science and technology of Great Britain and France after the Meiji Restoration of 1868; and after the Second World War it set about imitating American culture. Japan's growth to maturity would therefore appear to have been a one-way process: while borrowing from other countries around the world Japan has done not a thing to further the spread of its own culture to other countries.

Today, however, a whole range of Japanese products from transistor radios and televisions to cars is reaching every corner of the world, and there can now be very few people who are ignorant of the fact that there is a country called Japan somewhere on this planet. And yet there are still lots of people in other countries who seriously believe that even now in Japan samurai wear swords and ride in rickshaws. The reality of Japan today seems to be far from widely known about. It is known to exist but few know anything about it. Perhaps Japan really is a black hole.

Since Japan is little known about, it is often misunderstood in various ways. One of the most widespread of these misunderstandings is the belief that Japan had been a primitive country until the Meiji Restoration and that it only made a modern industurialized country of itself afterwards by making a successful job of borrowing and copying what it needed from the advanced cultures of Europe and North America. This belief is common in the developed countries and in the developing countries too, some of which are trying to take Japan as a model in order to transform themselves into modern states. It may be unavoidable that people in other countries should view Japan in this way, but the fact that most Japanese are themselves taught that Japan's modernization began after the Meiji Restoration certainly makes it easier for erroneous opinions of Japan to gain currency in other countries.

Japan's history, when carefully studied, reveals that Japan did not change overnight from being a primitive country to being a modern state. Japan was modernizing itself in its own way well before it came into close contact with Europe and North America. At the beginning of the eighteenth century, Kyoto, Edo (the old name for Tokyo) and Osaka were already the largest cities in the world.

Japanese industry was flourishing too, and the social and economic systems were going through a process of modernization as well. The educational system was particularly well developed, with the result that the literacy rate already passed fifty per cent. There was probably no other country in the world at the time that had such a high literacy rate. The fact is that Japan and the countries of western Europe developed into modern states quite independently of each other. Or, to use a biological metaphor, it can be said that they went through parallel processes of evolution.

Why should countries far removed from each other on opposite sides of the world have gone through parallel processes of evolution and developed into the same kind of country? It is a matter of great interest for us Japanese to examine the course of our history within the context of world history, and to compare Japan and the countries of North America and Europe as contemporary phenomena. Such a comparative approach might also serve to help people in foreign countries gain an understanding of Japan as it really is.

This book has been put together at the request of the Plaza Hotel with the aim of helping the overseas participants attending the HRI meeting in Japan in November 1983 to form an accurate understanding of Japan. Each short chapter relates to a different aspect of Japan's history and they have been written by a group of university teachers and researchers who have tried to fit Japanese history into the perspective of world history. This approach has brought into focus both the unique qualities of Japan and the Japanese and those they share with other peoples and other lands. I hope that it will enable the overseas participants to discover Japan as it really is and help us in our turn to become more international in our outlook.

UMESAO-Tadao

Contributors;

UMESAO-Tadao
Director-General, National Museum of Ethnology.
Ethnology, Comparative studies of civilizations.

KOYAMA-Shuzo
Associate professor, National Museum of Ethnology.
Prehistory.

TANI-Naoki
Lecturer, Osaka City University.
Urban history, Architectural history.

MORIYA-Takeshi
Associate professor, National Museum of Ethnology.
Japanese Culture.

SONODA-Hidehiro
Research assistant, Research Institute of Humanistic Studies, Kyoto University.
Social history of Japan.

YONEYAMA-Toshinao
Professor, Kyoto University.
Cultural anthropology.

Translation assisted by;

Peter Kornicki, Richard H. Lock

Photo credits;

Kyodo News Service, The Yomiuri Newspaper, Kinki Nippon Tourist Co., Ltd., The Institute of Japanese Culture and Tourism, The Kansai Electric Power Co., Ltd., Yushodo Bookseller Co., Ltd., Nagasaki Municipal Museum, Yuko Innami

Contents

1 An Island Country

The image that Japan has abroad is one of a small, isolated and strange island country but where did this image come from? The Japanese archipelago consists of the four main islands of Hokkaido, Honshu, Shikoku and Kyushu together with more than a thousand smaller islands, and its overall area is approximately 370,000 square kilometers. These islands are inhabited by more than a hundred million people. Edwin Reischauer, a former American ambassador to Japan, has stated that Japan's image is a misleading one and owes its existence to the readiness of Americans to compare Japan with their own country, China, the Soviet Union and other geographical giants. In his opinion, it should rather be said that Japan is a compact country on a par with such countries of western Europe as France, Gremany, Italy and Great Britain which established the pattern of the modern imperialistic nation.

According to statistics published by the United Nations, most countries in the world have an area is excess of 50,000 square kilometers, and more than half have an area that is anything up to 250,000 square kilometers. It follows from this that Japan is in the upper half in terms of its area and is by no means a small country.

It seems likely that Japan's reputation as a small country lacking in space comes from the way in which the geographical features of the country have necessitated an unusual distribution of the population. Japan is a mountainous and hilly country and seventy-two per cent of its land is covered with steep inclines which are not suitable for settled residence. For that reason, the

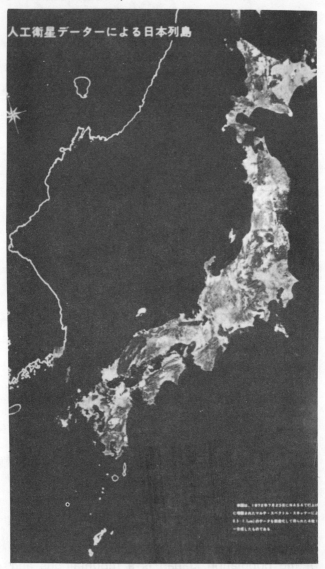

Japanese Archipelago filmed by an earth satellite (Kyodo)

agricultural lands are concentrated alongside the rivers or along the coastline, and it is there too that the population is to be found, packed tightly into small areas of land. Japan's overall population density is less than that of Belgium or the Netherlands, but in view of the fact that only about one quarter of Japan's area is usable, the actual population density is clearly considerably higher. Under such conditions as these, there is considerable population pressure, and psychological pressure also, on Japan's farming population. The farmers too, therefore, retain an image of Japan as a country lacking in space. The Meiji Restoration of 1868 put an end to more than 200 years of rigidly enforced national isolation, and hundreds of thousands of Japanese took the opportunity to emigrate to the United States, to Brazil, to Manchuria, and elsewhere. Most of them were farmers and they were placing their hopes on the possibility of being able to farm in wide open spaces.

And what of Japan's isolation? According to geologists and archaeologists, Japan was a part of the Asiatic mainland until the Ice Age. Animals of all kinds roamed over Japan, mammoths, deer and the brown bear from the north and the palaeooxodon and various species of deer from the south, and the animals were followed by men, who came and settled in what is now Japan. Fossils and archaeological remains provide ample proof of all this.

But with the end of the Ice Age temperatures began to rise, and so sea levels began to creep up. Some twelve thousand years ago the rising seas cut Japan off from the mainland and turned it into the group of islands it now is. The La Perouse strait separating Japan and Sakhalin is thus now 45 kilometers across and that between Japan and Korea some 200 kilometers. This put an end to the natural exchange of flora and fauna between Japan and the continent and of course an end to all human cultural contacts: henceforward these could only be accomplished with the help of shipbuilding and navigation.

On the Asiatic mainland the great civilization of China was already in existence. Over the centuries and millennia of its history China went through countless periods of unification and fragmentation, but during the periods when it was a unified state it had a tendency to expand and conquer, to the disadvantage of the surrounding nations. But Japan was separated from the mainland by two hundred kilometers of water and so only experienced Chinese military pressure during the Mongol invasions of the thirteenth century: otherwise, Japan was unscathed. This does not mean, however, that Japan lived in total isolation or was unable to achieve any cultural development, for it continued to dispatch envoys to the mainland and absorb the information they brought back with them. The straits separating Japan from the mainland thus helped Japan to avoid invasion or large scale immigration from the mainland while enabling it at the same time to maintain cultural, technological and intellectual contacts with it.

KOYAMA-Shuzo

⅟ Trees and Forests

There are four main areas of forest land in Japan. In the north in Hokkaido there are forests of needle-leaved evergreens, in the south, dividing Honshu into two parts, there are forests of broad-leaved deciduous trees and broad-leaved evergreens, and in the Ryukyu Islands there are tropical forests of broad-leaved evergreens. These correspond to the subarctic, cold temperate, temperate, and sub-tropical climatic zones respectively. In mountainous regions above two or three thousand metres there are further vegetational differences giving rise to alpine and alpestrine zones here and there. These distribution patterns were established after the end of the Ice Ages when temperatures became similar to those found now. Nevertheless, there have been some variations along the north-south axis brought about by alterations in the climatic conditions.

The relationship between man and his forests has followed similar patterns in most of the civilizations that developed in the temperate zones. One finds that in both Japan and Europe there have been periods when forest land has been used more or less as it is in its natural state, periods when forests have been cut down to clear land for cultivation or pastoral farming, and periods when forests have been cleared to make way for industrial growth. And in the future there will be a period when, in reaction to these trends, the emphasis is placed on the preservation of forest lands.

During the Jōmon period, when Japan was a hunting and gathering society, the cultural centre was in the east of the country. There, the deciduous forests consisted of Fagus crenata (the Japanese beech), Quercus crispula (a kind of oak) and chestnut trees, so there were broad spaces between the trees for the passage of sunlight, thus providing suitable conditions for a settled existence. The staple food was nuts, but deer and boar were hunted and eaten as well. Ninety percent of the archaeological remains dating from the Jōmon period are to be found in east Japan. Few are found from west Japan because the forests there were mostly of oak and so too dense to offer an acceptable form of existence to man or beast.

At the end of the Jōmon period the cultivation of cereals and rice was introduced from the continental mainland. These agricultural skills were mainly practised in areas of evergreen forest in the west of Japan, where the climate was much warmer. In the more mountainous areas, fields were burnt out of the woodland and secondary vegetation took the place of the forests. In the plains rice paddies were prepared and there most of the woodland disappeared in the course of time.

Because much of Japan is steep and hilly and the grasslands are difficult to maintain, and also because of the Buddhist prohibition on the taking of life, very little meat was eaten and so livestock-farming assumed no importance at all. For this reason destruction of the forest lands did not take place on any great scale. Also, under native forms of religious worship various mountains and forests were regarded as holy and sacred, and so large tracts of virgin forest remained intact throughout the country and were regarded as inviolable.

As the centuries passed and the population increased, towns developed, many wooden houses were built, and since the use of iron was becoming more common too, necessitating supplies of charcoal for the smelting process, the forest lands came under a good deal of pressure. The result of this was that in the Edo period only scanty secondary forests of red pine survived in some parts of western Japan and bare mountains became a common sight. Nevertheless, in general the power of the forests to replenish themselves was greater than the demands placed on them by human society and for the most part the forest lands were well preserved. This was because the feudal landowners learnt from experience that the preservation of the forests helped to prevent floods and the erosion of the land, and believed that a policy of preserving land and water supplies would contribute to greater harvests and so greater economic strength. In effect they were aware of the economic value of their forest lands, and for this reason they strove to nurture and protect them by, for example, placing limits on felling and lumbering activities. In terms of results, policies of this sort served the same function as did the determination of feudal landowners in Europe to preserve their forest lands for hunting.

Recent statistics show that forest lands now occupy 70% of Japan's total land area, a percentage that is close to that found in the countries of Scandinavia. When one recalls that the percentage for the whole world is a mere 30%, it is clear that Japan is blessed with a high percentage of forest lands. But the rate per individual me.nber of the population stands at 0.24 hectares and this cannot be said to be a high one. Also, it is particularly noticeable that the area of woodland in the towns and cities of Japan is small. The expansion of the cities at the expense of the surrounding forests in recent years and the destruction of the natural environment in the mountainous areas owing to the construction of golf courses, ski resorts and tourists facilities of all kinds have been startling.

The forest lands in Japan today cover steep slopes that do not lend themselves to easy access and are mixtures of many different kinds of trees, so they do not have a great contribution to make in terms of raw materials. It is for this reason that lumber for the building industry, woodchips and pulp are currently being imported from America, Canada, the Soviet Union, Indonesia and many other countries.

KOYAMA-Shuzo

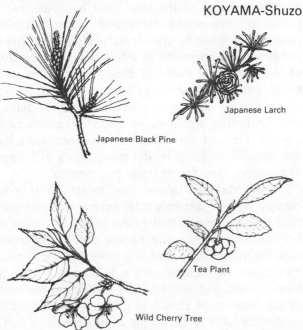

Japanese Larch

Japanese Black Pine

Tea Plant

Wild Cherry Tree

1 The Four Seasons

In Japan there are clear differences between each of the four seasons, and the Japanese are said to be a people unusually sensitive to changes in nature. As the seasons change, Japanese are accustomed to changing their modes of dress and their household ornaments, enjoying the foods of the season, and appreciating the changes in the natural landscape. The changes of the seasons, however, do not bring only pleasure, for they also bring with them typhoons, floods and blizzards, and the damage these cause makes it look sometimes as if the fury of the gods has been unleashed. The Japanese haiku is one of the shortest poetic forms, but in each haiku there is without fail some word that expresses or indicates the season. These words refer to such things as annual festivals, flowers, birds or insects, all associated with a particular time of year, and they have even been collected together into reference works for poets. A sense of the seasons is also very important in the practice of ikebana, or flower arrangement, and tea ceremony.

The Japanese archipelago extends from north to south, and the northern tip of Hokkaido lies at a latitude of about 45 degrees north, while the southern tip of Kyushu lies at a latitude of 30 degrees north, with the Ryukyu islands further to the south. Thus it ranges from the latitude of Venice to that of Cairo, or, in North American terms, from the latitude of Montreal to that of Florida. In terms of latitude, then, Japan is more to the south than most countries of the civilized northern hemisphere. So Japan naturally has summers that are hot and humid. The traditional Japanese house made of bamboo and paper seems ideally suited to this sort of climate. The winters, however, are extremely cold, and the average temperature in Tokyo in January is lower than that of Reykjavik in Iceland, which is some twenty-eight degrees of latitude further to the north.

Why should Japan have such a climate as this, when it is an island country and should enjoy an oceanic climate? The probable explanation is that owing to Japan's proximity to the mainland of Asia its climate is heavily influenced by that of the mainland, which is of course a continental climate. Thus Japan's climate is controlled by the combined workings of the continental and Pacific Ocean air masses, as will now be made clear.

During the winter months of December to February, the climate is under the control of the high pressure areas of the Siberian continental air mass, at the centre of which is a large mass of cold air stretching from Lake Baikal to the Mongolian border. Periodic cold waves flow down to Japan from this air mass, lowering the temperatures all over Japan. Also, seasonal winds from central Siberia cross the Japan Sea where warm air currents are flowing northwards; there they absorb large amounts of moisture, which is deposited as snow on the mountainous areas of Japan. Japan is in fact a country with one of the heaviest snow falls in the world, so the mountains are full of ski resorts, which attract holiday-makers from the cities in large numbers at the beginning and end of each year. Skiing is one of the most popular sports in Japan and the skiing population of Japan far exceeds that of the European Alpine countries.

During the summer months of June, July and August, on the other hand, Japan is much affected by high pressure areas coming in from the Pacific. Towards Siberia on the continent there are low pressure areas at this time of year, and the air streams flow from west to east and south to north, bringing lots of heat and moisture to Japan. The index of discomfort is based on temperature and humidity and when the figure of eighty is exceeded (65% humidity and 30 degrees C - 86F), everybody experiences some discomfort. During the summer in Tokyo and Osaka, most days exceed this figure.

There is a rainy season at the start of summer. Cold currents of air from the high pressure areas of the Sea of Okhotsk flow down to Japan and clash with the warm, moist currents of air from the South Pacific high pressure areas to form the rainy season; this lingers to produce a spell of rainy weather and the small low pressure areas give rise to heavy rainfalls. This of course makes rice cultivation possible in Japan, but it also causes damage from time to time, when floods or

Typhoon filmed by a meteorological satellite

landslides occur.

In September and October there is a special meteorological phenomenon in the form of the typhoon. Typhoons are defined as winds that are produced in tropical low-pressure areas in the southern oceans near the equator and have a wind speed at the centre of seventeen metres per second. They frequently cause great damage like the hurricanes of the Atlantic, the cyclones of the Indian Ocean, and the willy-willies of Australia, but they are also a valuable phenomenon in that they bring large amounts of rain.

Spring (March to May) and Autumn (September to November) are times when the continental and oceanic air masses change places over Japan. There are some sharp climatic changes but in general the temperature is warm and the climate is temperate during these seasons. Since ancient times the Japanese people have found spring and autumn the most delightful and comfortable seasons.

As explained above, the Japanese climate is in general a warm and damp one, though with severe winters and fierce summers. Western Europe and the coasts of North America also share a climate such as this, and it may well be that this sort of climate provides the ideal conditions for industrial development, cultural growth and the advance of modern capitalistic society in general.

KOYAMA-Shuzo

1 The Oldest Pots in the World

The making of earthenware vessels probably developed after the chance discovery that earth in the vicinity of fire underwent some changes on exposure to heat, and this technological development is generally regarded as an indication, along with the development of agriculture, of the advent of the New Stone Age. Until recently it was thought that the art of making pottery developed in Mesopotamia and then spread throughout the world. In the East it spread to India and China, and in China about five thousand years ago it led to the emergence of two different kinds of pottery, one the coloured pottery of Yanshao culture and the other the black, rough, straw-rope-patterned pottery that appears to have been made in the provinces.

In the Jōmon period (up until 200 BC) in Japan's early history, much use was made of pots decorated with cord-marking ('Jōmon' is the word for it in Japanese), and it had been supposed from the overall physical similarities that the making of these pots in Japan had been stimulated by the importation of Chinese cord-marked pottery. But in 1965 the carbon dating method was developed which enabled an objective and absolute method of dating to take the place of the methods used hitherto, which had relied on the comparison of shapes, decorations, and so on.

Following the introduction of this new method, work began on the re-examination of archaeological remains and in 1969 tests found that pottery discovered in the Natsushima shell-mound in Kanagawa Prefecture was seven thousand years old, making it the oldest in the world. This did great harm to the theory that traditional Japanese earthenware had come over from the Chinese mainland, and for a while the academic world was split over the issue.

As time passed, the results of more and more carbon 14 dating tests came to light and they confirmed not only the great age of Jōmon pottery but also the hypothesis that had been put forward earlier concerning the order in which different kinds of Jōmon pottery had first made their appearance. A number of items are now known to be about ten thousand years old, the oldest being between twelve and thirteen thousand years old, thus pushing still further back the beginnings of pottery in Japan. In some cases these pots are found in company with stone implements from the Old Stone Age, but since remains of the same age from the continent have so far yielded no pottery at all, it is evident that Japanese pottery evolved independently. The oldest finds of pottery outside Japan have been made in Turkey and are eight thousand six hundred years old, so Japanese pottery is clearly the oldest that has so far been discovered in the world.

The great age of Jōmon pottery has attracted the interest of archaeologists from all over the world, and it has been suggested that Jōmon pottery may even have spread from Japan to South America. At the Valdivia site in Ecuador, it has been discovered that some four thousand years ago local culture suddenly acquired knowledge of pottery-making. The pots are well-finished and have unusual decorative patterns made using shells, which were either impressed into or scratched across the clay. They are of a high standard and it can only be concluded that they were not developed there but brought in from outside. After comparing these pots with other remains from the region, the archaeologists who were working on the site concluded that, taking into account both the date and level of technology, they most probably came from Kyushu in Japan, on the other side of the Pacific.

It is known that even in the Jōmon period dug-out canoes were in use in Japan, and excavation of shell-mounds has yielded the remains of large, deep-sea fish such as tuna as well as of whales. So it would appear that Jōmon people were well adapted to the ocean environment. Therefore the hypothesis is that one or more Jōmon people in dugouts on the open sea were caught in a typhoon and blown to the middle of the Pacific, from where they were carried to the North or South American coastline by the strong easterly ocean currents in that part of the Pacific. Close examination of records relating to ships adrift in the Pacific has revealed that with good fortune it would have been possible to get from Japan to Ecuador in just over a month. It is now thought that there is a strong possibility that one or more Jōmon people did do just that.

This hypothesis relies heavily on a number of chance factors and it cannot be said that it commands wide academic support as yet. But it does have its attractions, especially as a theory prompted by the great age of pottery-making in Japan.

Earthenware pots have continued to be used throughout Japan's history, as is clear from the fact that they constitute the most common and numerous items found in archaeological sites throughout Japan. The earliest pots were probably used only for boiling water, but as the number of uses multiplied, so too did the variety of shapes and decorative techniques. The more refined pots of the Jōmon period are light and thin, carefully decorated and finished with a black polish so that they look like metal. The level of technology that they exhibit can be said to be high indeed.

As Japan came to have more and more contact with the mainland, the potter's wheel, the kiln, porcelain and pottery dyeing techniques were introduced to Japan. Japanese potters added further improvements of their own to these imports and produced technology of porcelain-making that was unique to Japan, with the result that Japan became one of the leading producers of porcelain in the world. The modern porcelain industry has moved a step beyond the stage of simply making pottery and works of art from clay, and it is now involved in the manufacture of new ceramics made out of titanium, silicon and other new materials. It has thus become an industry closely connected with electronics and space exploration, but the traditions on which it rests go back to the Jōmon period.

KOYAMA-Shuzo

Imari—Major porcelain-making district

1 What Our Ancestors Left Behind

Shell-mounds are the name given to the rubbish heaps left by early man. They consist mainly of broken household implements and food remains, especially the shells of shell-fish. Shell-mounds dating from the New Stone Age onwards are found all over the world, for by that time many communities had learnt to live off the sea.

It was an American, the zoologist Edward Sylvester Morse, who was the first to carry out

scientific investigations into the shell-mounds of Japan. In 1877 he excavated a shell-mound at Omori in the vicinity of Tokyo and the following year he published a detailed report on his findings. Morse was one of those who had accepted the theory of evolution, which was an advanced position to adopt at that time. He knew a lot about the excavations and investigations of shell-mounds that were currently being carried out in Denmark and elsewhere and he himself had been involved in the excavation of shell-mounds in Florida.

As a result of his excavations of the Omori shell-mound, Morse drew a number of interesting conclusions. He said that there had once been in Japan a people who had made earthenware vessels with a rope- or chain-like pattern and that they had eaten shell-fish, fish and various kinds of meat. These people, he said, had not been Japanese but people similar to the Ainu, albeit an older race of people who could be described as pre-Ainu people. The name now given to the age in which these people lived and produced their pottery is the Jōmon period (jōmon means rope-pattern) and it refers to the period up to about 200 BC during which earthenware pottery with this unique kind of pattern was made and when the predominating economy was based on hunting and gathering.

More than two thousand shell-mounds are known in Japan today and most of them date from the Jōmon period. The majority of the sites containing shell-mounds are large in size and the settlements appear to have been there a long time. It is supposed that the people living on these sites had a relatively high degree of the requisite technology for gathering their food and seeing to their other needs from the sea and the surrounding area. Thus even the older shell-mounds contain pieces of basic fishing equipment such as barbed spears and sinkers for use with fishing nets, and subsequent generations would simply have improved on the workmanship and design of these pieces of equipment.

Some of the shell-mounds dating from the late Jōmon period contain large numbers of just a single kind of shell. Some scholars think that these may have been places where shells were turned into a primitive form of currency, but it is also possible to suppose that by this time there were already fishermen who had become specialists in a particular kind of catch.

The use of the resources offered by the sea and the seashore continued even after the shift to agricultural patterns of life. This was because fish continued to provide a large part of the animal protein consumed by Japanese. Japan could not provide enough protein in the form of meat because of the mountainous nature of its terrain and the high population density which had resulted from the introduction of rice cultivation. To meet the demand, special fishing villages developed alongside rivers and by the sea which acted as suppliers of fish to inland towns and villages.

Specialization of this kind was certainly in existence by the eighth century, and it is clear from written records that by this time some processing of fish and shell-fish was also being carried out, mainly involving preservation in salt and drying. From around the fourteenth century onwards such products of the sea as sea cucumbers and abalone came to play an important part in Japan's trade with China.

Japanese have long been interested in the products of the sea, and this is nowhere more apparent than in Japanese cuisine. At the centre of that cuisine is sashimi, fresh fish that is eaten raw, the preparation and serving of which can only be described as artistic.

The Japanese fishing industry today is among the most successful in the world. Since 1972 it has been producing big catches amounting to ten million tons, about twenty per cent of the world total. Most of the fish caught come from the seas around Japan, but some twenty per cent is brought home by deep-sea fishing vessels that travel as far as the seas off the USA, South and Central America, South-East Asia and Africa. Some Japanese fisheries have also joined up with foreign fisheries to form joint enterprises, and Japan also imports a great deal of fish from other countries, particularly quality fish like bonito, tuna, chameleon prawns and roe. So at the same time as being a major fishing nation, Japan is also a major importer of fish.

Fish and shell-fish account for between forty and fifty per cent of Japanese consumption of animal protein. That this is a high figure becomes apparent when comparison is made with such countries as the United States and New Zealand, where fish accounts for less than five per cent of animal protein consumed, and even with Spain, the Soviet Union and Denmark, where the figure is around twenty per cent. The consumption of fish and shell-fish is declining in Japan owing to the recent trends in favour of meat consumption, but since the Japanese have a tradition of fish-eating that is some ten thousand years old, it is likely that fish will remain an important part of the Japanese diet for the forseeable future.

KOYAMA-Shuzo

1 Living off Nuts

In shops and markets today, many different kinds of nuts are on sale, including chestnuts, walnuts, hazelnuts, almonds and cashew nuts. They are mostly used as snacks, to accompany drinks, and in cooking and cake-making. However, in the plant-gathering era before the cultivation of cereals became widespread, it was very common for nuts to be used as a staple food. Archaeological finds have revealed that hazelnuts were available in northern Europe and acorns and pistachio nuts were available throughout the orient. Also, the Californian Indians used acorns as a staple food, and in Micronesia, Melanesia, Polynesia and other islands in the southern Pacific nuts still have an important role to play in supplementing sweet potatoes, which are the staple food.

Archaeological remains from the Jōmon era in Japan (from earliest times until about 200 B.C.) show that walnuts, chestnuts, horse chestnuts and many different kinds of acorn were used as foods in Japan in the distant past. Walnuts and chestnuts can be eaten raw, but acorns and horse chestnuts contain bitter tannin and saponin and cannot be eaten unless some method is developed for removing the bitter flavour. And in fact it seems that at first only walnuts and chestnuts were used as food in Japan, while horse chestnuts and acorns did not come to be used widely until about six thousand years ago.

The art of removing the bitter taste from horse chestnuts and acorns survives to this day in Japanese country villages. In the autumn when the nuts are ripe, the villagers or groups go into the mountains to gather the nuts. To preserve the acorns they have gathered, they dry them in front of a fire. Next they remove the hard skin, pound the nuts to pieces and then leave them to soak in running water for as long as a week. Then the nuts are placed in hot water, with lye sometimes added as a neutralizer, and boiled for more than twenty-four hours with constant changes of water. Once the pieces have been dried, they are then reduced to powder. The powder is finally eaten as a kind of starch-paste which is used to make rice cakes (mochi) or dumplings(dango). The technique of leaving the nuts in running water is also found in Indian society in California, and there may well have been connections between Indian society and the Jōmon culture of Japan.

In order for a particular foodstuff to play the role of a staple food, the most important consid-

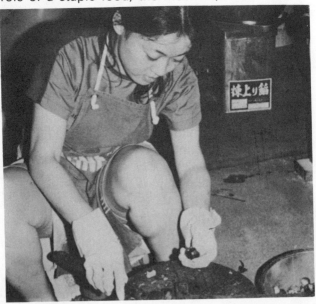

Making chestnut mochi

eration is that it be available in sufficient quantities. The technique of leaving nuts in running water was a revolutionary one which made it possible to make effective use not only of the walnuts, chestnuts and other nuts which can be eaten raw, but also of the acorns which grow in large quantities on the Quercus (oak) throughout the Japanese forest lands. The starch contained in the nuts can easily be preserved by drying, and this makes for a stable food supply which is independent of seasonal factors.

The acorn starch obtained through the process of soaking the acorns in water is an effective source of calories but contains virtually no proteins or fats, and so it has some shortcomings when used as food. To compensate for this, it was necessary to hunt and fish on a large scale. For this reason it is supposed that in Jōmon period society there was a clear division of labour between the sexes, with the women's role being the plant-gathering to keep up a supply of a source of calories and the men's role being the hunting and fishing which was necessary to guarantee a source of protein and fats. Once economic organization along these lines had come into existence, Jōmon society made rapid development. The amount of archaeological remains increases, and it is apparent that centres of population form on a large scale and exhibit a high degree of permanence. At the centre of these settlements was a town square around which the dwellings were arranged. There is also an increase in the number of surviving ceremonial implements, such as earthen figures and shaped pieces of stone, and in some cases these are even found being worshipped in each house in a settlement. And the emergence of social classes is suggested by the discovery in graves of earrings made from precious stones and bracelets made of rare shells. Moreover, it also seems that regional trade was being carried out as well on a substantial scale. This is clear from the discovery in many sites of obsidian stone implements which had been brought far from their place of origin. Jōmon society reached the peak of its prosperity about four thousand years ago and was centred in eastern Japan. Archaeological remains suggest that the population at that time was about 270,000 and that the average population density in, for example, the central mountainous districts, was as high as three per square kilometre.

Later, when the techniques of the slash-and-burn method of agriculture and rice cultivation were brought through to Japan, Jōmon society managed to adapt to the new agricultural techniques without being thrown into social turmoil, and it went on to make further cultural development. Such development was possible because the cultural pre-conditions were fulfilled: it was a society which was divided into classes and which had been able to adapt to an agricultural economy instead of the simpler forest economy based on nut-gathering it had been practising hitherto, it knew about the cultivation of plants, and it had made considerable technological progress.

KOYAMA-Shuzo

How the Japanese took to Rice

Japan, now a highly industrialized country with a large population, relies on imports for its supplies of wheat, soya beans, fruits and many other foodstuffs. However, in the case of rice, which is the staple food of Japan, imports are unnecessary for sufficient quantities are produced at home.

If one travels by rail or road into the country between the end of April and June, one sees paddy fields full of water stretching out in every direction, interrupted here and there only by compact clusters of houses. Since Japan has little flat land, gently sloping hillsides are also converted into paddies for rice cultivation. So to the traveller in the countryside the appearance is not unlike that of many of the monsoon countries of Asia.

Rice is, however, not native to Japan. It was first cultivated thousands of years ago in tropical Asia and it is thought to have reached Japan either directly from southern China or via the Korean peninsula. The introduction of rice cultivation enabled Japan to shift from a society dependent on hunting and gathering to an agricultural society. The new age that emerged on this agricultural basis is called the Yayoi period (ca. 200BC to ca 250 AD).

Rice cultivation first spread widely through western Japan and then spread steadily northwards. By the eighth century it was more or less established in all the regions of Japan with a warm climate, that is to say, not in Hokkaido. Rice was originally a tropical crop and so it has poor resistance to cold, but efforts continued to be made to cultivate it in colder soil, and so the northern frontier of the rice-producing areas of Japan was gradually pushed further and further to the north. It was only about one hundred years ago that rice was first cultivated in Hokkaido, but Hokkaido has now become one of the major rice-producing areas of Japan. Northern Hokkaido lies at the northern limit of world rice cultivation, around latitude 45 degrees north.

Rice and Japanese culture have long enjoyed a close relationship. First and foremost, rice has for more than two thousand years been the staple food of the Japanese. It is rich in calories and contains a comparatively large amount of vegetable protein as well as substantial amounts of vitamins, phosphorus, iron and so on. It is thus an excellent foodstuff, supplying most of man's nutritional needs. The Japanese diet came to depend on large quantities of boiled rice as the staple food (or, alternatively, barley or other cereals), with small amounts of fish or vegetables as the main dish, and also miso soup, made from fermented soya beans. This combination of rice and fish provides a diet that is low in both calories and cholesterol and in this respect the Japanese diet differs markedly from Western diets which are based on meat. In America some attention is now being paid to the Japanese diet as a model diet for greater health and the prevention of such conditions of middle age as obesity.

Rice can support a comparatively large population. Since it requires paddy fields for its cultivation, there is little need for fertilizers and it is possible to produce crops from the same field year after year. When one compares this with the agricultural practices of Europe, where crops are rotated and fields are left to lie fallow, since it is impossible to cultivate barley on the same field year after year, it is clear that the productive capacity of rice for a given area of land is much greater. This has made it possible for Japan to be entirely self-sufficient in rice in spite of the fact that the geography of Japan makes it impossible for more than fifteen per cent of the land to be used for agriculture. As a result of this combination of circumstances, by the beginning of the nineteenth century Japan had a population of thirty-five million with the comparatively high population density of one hundred people per square kilometre.

Rice has also had an important role to play in Japan as a form of currency. In the eighth century Japan was divided into sixty-eight administrative districts, or provinces. The reputations of these districts depended on the amounts of rice they could produce, and of course their taxes were paid in rice. This arrangement persisted until the Meiji period, when a modern currency system took its place. During the Edo period these administrative districts were further subdivided, but the domains of the feudal lords were in the same way held to be valuable to the extent that the land they contained produced good yields of rice. The stipends of the retainers of these lords were also paid in rice.

Nevertheless, there was also a money economy which had developed before the beginning of the Edo period among people of the merchant class, who controlled the distribution and marketing networks of Japan. So there existed two parallel but related systems, the rice economy of the samurai and the farmers, and the money economy of merchants and the artisans.

The most important task facing the person at

the head of any administrative unit was the raising of the level of rice production within the area under his authority. Since the society of the Edo period was based on hereditary succession of occupation, this task was crucial for the maintenance of the livelihood of his family and retainers. Therefore the promotion of agriculture and especially rice production became the basis of administrative policy. In this regard irrigation was of prime importance and throughout Japan many major works were undertaken under government auspices, some involving the construction of river embankments, others the digging of ditches to distribute water around the fields; and the result of all this was that paddy fields eventually covered every available inch of space in the country.

At the same time, farmers were constantly striving for technological advancement. They made improvements to their tools and equipment, and sought to select grain varieties that would be suitable for early planting, late planting and planting in cold areas. The result of these efforts was a rice-yield per acre that is now the highest in the world.

After the Meiji Restoration of 1868, the technology and techniques of Japanese rice cultivation spread overseas as emigrants left Japan for the United States and Brazil. Thanks to their initial efforts, California is now one of the leading rice-producing areas in the world.

KOYAMA-Shuzo

⅃Where They Came From

The Japanese are a sub-group of the Mongoloid peoples who inhabit large parts of Asia and the New World. This is evident from such characteristics of the Japanese as the following: a skin colour that is pale to light brown; straight black hair; brown eyes; a relative lack of body hair; and a high frequency of such features as epicantic eyes, the mongoloid spot (a spot found in the caudal area at the base of the spine in infancy) and shovel-shaped incisors.

The Japanese differ widely, however, from individual to individual in matters of facial characteristics and physical features. They have no unifying characteristic as a people, and they are variously said to resemble such Asiatic peoples as the Indonesians, the Thais, the Cambodians and the Koreans.

Since the early Stone Age there have been racial pressures in Asia as people moved from inland areas to the coasts and these population movements also exerted some influence on Japan. Geographically, though, Japan was the end of the line of migration and there was nowhere to move on to from Japan. It is therefore widely supposed that the Japanese race was formed over a long period of time by the mingling of successive waves of migrants to the Japanese archipelago from the continental mainland.

Recent anthropological research, however, has revealed that racial characteristics which were considered hitherto to be unchanging, such as the cranial index, do undergo some evolution and go through changes. To give some examples, during the thirty years since the end of the Second World War, the average height of the Japanese has grown by about ten centimetres, the Japanese have become more dolichocephalic and their noses have become more prominent. These changes are largely thought to be due to changes in eating habits and a trend towards westernized patterns of life, exemplified by the increased consumption of meat and dairy products.

It appears less likely, therefore, to some that the emergence of the Japanese as a race was the result of large scale population movements and subsequent changes in physical characteristics. The alternative theory put forward is that there was an original population of the Japanese islands during the Stone Age and that this original population developed into the modern Japanese with various admixtures from other races along the way.

Fossilized human remains found throughout the Japanese archipelago indicate that in the Old Stone Age, when Japan was still physically connected to the mainland, there were two different peoples living in different parts of the country, one with a small frame and of light build, and the other of sturdier physique. Many thousands of human bones have been found from the Jōmon period following the Stone Age, and from these it has been demonstrated that early Jōmon man was small and of light build, but that from the middle of the Jōmon period onwards Jōmon man was sturdier in build. To explain these changes, two theories have been put forward, one attributing the changes to nutritional improvements and the other to racial differences. The latter theory is based on the view that the sturdier of the two Stone Age groups became the dominant one.

But, generally speaking, what seems to have happened is this. As a result of the separation of Japan from the mainland, a comparatively uniform race came into being with many of the physical characteristics of earlier peoples. The great changes in the physical characteristics of the Japanese seem to have emerged later, during the Yayoi period when the Japanese ceased from being hunters and gatherers and moved to agriculture. Yayoi man was taller than Jōmon man, his jaw was less prominent, and he was longer and flatter in face. These characteristics were most pronounced in the people living on the coasts of western Japan, which is the part nearest to the Asiatic mainland, but they were also found in eastern Japan and in the mountainous areas of Japan. So while it is possible to explain these changes as being due to racial mixture occasioned by large-scale migration from the continent, another view also demands some attention, namely the view that places more emphasis on the acquisition of a stable source of food and the nutritional improvement which were both brought about by agricultural developments and especially by the introduction of rice cultivation. Nevertheless, during the centuries between the early formation of the nation state in the Yayoi period and the completion of this process in the seventh century, there was a lot of contact between Japan and Korea and the mainland, and it is quite conceivable that there was some racial mixing with the people who were continually migrating to Japan at this time, albeit not in large numbers.

One of the most interesting ethnic groups in the Japanese archipelago is the Ainu. The Ainu have distinct physical characteristics such as pale skin, hairy bodies and clear-cut features. Many theories have been put forward to explain their ethnic origins, such as that they are Caucasoid or are remnants of an ancient race, but their origins have long remained cloaked in mystery. Recently, however, a number of interesting discoveries have been made, such as the fact that they lack the marker genes which are a feature of caucasian peoples. And it would appear from computer analysis of their cranial measurements that the Ainu were Jōmon people who lived geographically isolated lives on Hokkaido and persisted there with a hunting and gathering way of life and that, although originally a Jōmon people of Mongoloid stock, they went through a different process of evolution from that which led to the emergence of the Japanese as they are today.

KOYAMA-Shuzo

At 'Sanja Festival' in Asakusa, Tokyo

Burying the Dead

In the third century B.C.' China was unified under the Ch'in dynasty, and it developed under the Former Han Dynasty into a great empire that in the west bordered on the Roman Empire. But on the edges of and around the Chinese empire there were many nomadic or seafaring people whose ways of life differed from those of Chinese society, which was largely based on agriculture.These peoples formed their own small states which maintained contacts with China; sometimes these relations were essentially tributary, and at other times relations were more hostile. There was a tradition in China, each time a dynasty came to an end, of compiling a record of its history, and these records often contain detailed information about the customs and culture of these small states on the periphery of the Chinese empire.

According to the sections of these records relating to Japan, there were lots of small states in Japan at the beginning of the Christian era, and they were frequently at war with each other. But, in the second century A.D. a queen called Himiko brought the wars to an end and established a unified nation. This was the prototype of the modern Japanese state. The records state that Himiko's state was called Yamatai, but it is not possible now to say with any certainty where it was located: many theories have been put forward, and the two most likely areas are Kyushu and the area around present-day Nara.

When Himiko died, the records state, a large mound was constructed more than a hundred paces in diameter, and more than one hundred slaves were buried with her. Current archaeological opinion has it that although no burial mound has yet come to light to correspond with this description, many large mounds have been found which date from about a century later and fit closely with the description in the Chinese records. The most interesting of these has a sort of keyhole shape - rounded at one end but squared off at the other end - that is unique to Japan and that is also quite different from the round or square mounds traditionally constructed in China and Korea. The earliest of these keyhole-shaped mounds are the largest and they are found concentrated around Nara, Kyoto, and Osaka. Many of them are regarded as the tombs of direct ancestors of the present imperial family. From the fifth century onwards the keyhole-shaped mounds spread to Kyushu and north-eastern Japan: they are found in groups of many different shapes and sizes, but it is supposed from their general large size and the presence of many funerary objects deposited inside them that they were the tombs of powerful local families. The construction of these large tombs would have required not only a considerable amount of power in order to assemble work force of sufficient size, but also a measurement system for the planning and construction itself. Recent research has demonstrated that the plan for the keyhole-shaped mounds was based upon a two-dimensional representation of a triangle superimposed on a circle, which was then translated into three-dimensional shape, so it is apparent that by this stage the builders had command of the requisite engineering and surveying skills based on a knowledge of geometry. It therefore seems reasonable to suppose that the keyhole-shaped tombs were symbols of the power and authority

Mausoleum dedicated to Emperor Nintoku (Kyodo)

granted by the court to powerful families in the provinces who had sworn submission to it, and at the same time examples of the level to which construction engineering had reached by then.

The largest keyhole-shaped tomb is that of Emperor Nintoku (d. 399), which lies in the middle of the plain within the boundaries of Sakai City in Osaka Prefecture. It is 486 metres long, 305 metres wide at its widest point, and 33.6 metres high, and it is surrounded by a double moat. It covers an area of 485 square metres, and it would have required some 1,400,000 cubic metres of earth for its construction. It was therefore on a bigger scale and would have required more labour than either the pyramids at Giza, which are said to have taken twenty years to complete, or the Chinese imperial tombs.

Recently some restoration work has been done

on a tomb within the boundaries of Kobe City. The tomb is 194 metres long, which is of medium size for a keyhole-shaped tomb. After excavations had been completed, attempts were made to re-create the tomb as it had once been by covering it with stones and 2200 pieces of broken pottery and ornaments. The whole undertaking took ten years and 250 million yen.

The ancient tombs of Japan may be seen as symbols of the autocratic, sovereign state that Japan was at that time, but their appearance was probably made possible by the introduction and spread of rice cultivation. The population of the Kinki area, which centres on present-day Osaka and Nara and is particularly rich in burial mounds, was about forty thousand when a hunting and gathering economy was predominant, and this figure suggests a population density of 0.13 people per square kilometre; by the second century, when rice cultivation had established itself in Japan, the population was about 110,000 with a population density of 3.33 per square kilometre; and by the seventh century the population was more than one million. This illustrates the ability of agriculture based on rice to support a large population, but these rapid increases in population also suggest that the technology for the cultivation of rice did not simply progress naturally but was probably given active encouragement as a matter of policy. Irrigation works were the principal form this encouragement took. And so the great tombs towering up in the plains are symbols of the technology and power of a society that had the capacity to undertake such large scale engineering works, and also constitute an ostentatious display of that power.

KOYAMA-Shuzo

From Bronze to Iron

Metal implements first made their appearance in Japan after the introduction of rice cultivation and it seems most likely that bronze and iron were actually introduced from the Korean penisula at more or less the same time in the middle of the second century B.C.. Until stone tools were eventually abandoned, they continued to be used alongside the new bronze and iron implements for a while. Iron was used for making farming tools and weapons because of the ease with which it could be given a sharp edge, while bronze, which could easily be formed or moulded into shapes, was used for making religious and ceremonial objects.

In Japan it was first bronze that came to be widely used, and it was only later that iron came into use. In China at this time iron was already in widespread use and iron tools had replaced bronze tools, with the result that excess bronze was available for neighbouring countries, and it is thought that these circumstances affected Japan and led to an initial period in which bronze was widely used. Most early Japanese bronze objects are in fact of Chinese or Korean origin, and they were more practical and more skillfully worked than later bronze objects made in Japan. The discovery in a number of locations in Japan of workshops and moulds dating from round about the beginning of the Christian era reveal that by that time bronze objects were being produced in Japan as well.

Most of the bronze objects made in Japan at that time had no practical value at all. Thus the swords that were made may have been large but they were too thin to be of any use as weapons. Bronze bells made at that time are said to have been modelled on horse bells but they are sometimes well over a metre in size, the decoration is usually Japanese, and they have altogether lost the character of bells that are hung up to be rung. Swords and bells of this type are often discovered by themselves in the mountains or under large stones far removed from settlements and burial places and they seem to have fulfilled the role of magical objects used by village communities to serve as prayers for good harvests. The distribution patterns of the swords and bells used for such purposes are by no means identical, for the swords are found in western Japan and especially in Kyushu while the bells are found to the east in the Kinki region, which is centred around Nara.

During the Tumulus period in the fourth century when the Yamato court was established in the Kinki region, these bronze swords and bells suddenly stopped being produced any more. The swords were replaced by ones made of iron, and their religious functions were taken over by bronze mirrors, which became the main ritual objects placed in tumuli at the time of burial. These mirrors are round in shape and said to symbolize the sun. What may well lie behind the appearance of these mirrors, then, is the subjugation of a weaker group using the bell as its symbol by a new and stronger group which had a form of sun worship, for the emperor was known as 'Child of the Sun'.

In the beginning, iron was used only for objects with a practical value. The first iron implements were such comparatively small farming tools as knives, hoes and so on. At first, these were brought over from the Korean peninsula as ready-made objects, but it was not long before they came to be made in Japan, too. In the section of the chronicle *Gishiwajinden* relating to a kingdom in Korea, the following passage appears. 'Many people come from Japan and from other kingdoms in Korea to get the iron which is made here. Iron is widely used in trade just like a form of currency'. So it appears that by the third century the Japanese had passed beyond the stage of merely importing iron objects and were now journeying to the continent to buy the raw materials which they would then bring back to Japan for forging and processing there. In Japan, the processing of iron took the form not so much of casting as of forging in small-scale workshops. The tradition of forging later bore fruit in the form of the Japanese sword, which attained the level of an object of art. In Japan, iron was obtained from iron sand, but the technology for its extraction was not developed until the sixth century.

Because Japanese iron manufacturing at this time was based on forging, many small-scale workshops developed in various parts of the country, often run just by one or two people. These manufacturers of iron objects moved from place to place in search of the necessary iron sand and the wood and charcoal that were used as fuel, and they became a social group providing a service for the farmers. They had a secret organization rather like that of the freemasons in Europe. Thus, the remains of many iron workshops are found in the mountains somewhat distant from the farming villages.

Japanese forging skills improved with the passage of time, and by the fifteenth century Japanese swords had become a major export item in the trade between Japan and China. And within a few years of the introduction of guns to Japan, the Japanese were making their own guns and later even forging their own cannons.

About two thousand years ago, the Japanese society rapidly became stratified and a social system developed, which consisted of large numbers of peasants and a ruling class with the emperor at its head. This process was not, of course, an entirely peaceful one and there were undoubtedly many struggles on the way. The large-scale production of iron weapons played an important role here and the powerful families were the ones with access to large quantities of weapons. Tumuli dating from this time often contain weapons and other pieces of military equipment made of iron, especially in the Kinki region and around the Inland Sea.

In Japan, when an emperor ascends to the throne, he receives a set of three divine objects consisting of a mirror, sword, and jewel. These are said to have been given by the gods to the ancestor of the emperor when he came to rule on earth, and the mirror is said to symbolize the sun, the sword to symbolize fighting power, and the jewel to symbolize water and food production. The development of early Japanese technology is reflected in the fact that these three objects are made of bronze, iron, and stone, but they can also be thought to symbolize the three classes of rulers, warriors, and peasants.

KOYAMA-Shuzo

Japan Becomes Buddhist

Buddhism was founded in India by Shakyamuni in the fourth century B.C. and developed out of the polytheistic Hindu religion. Whereas Hinduism remained more or less within the boundaries of India, Buddhism spread extensively and reached Sri Lanka, the countries of South-East Asia, the lands to the west of China, Mongolia, China, Korea and Japan.

Buddhism is characterised by its lack of a single written source of doctrinal authority, by the great changes it has undergone over the ages, by its complicated doctrine, and by its insistence on a basic rule of life which requires the avoidance of evil and the purification of one's own heart and mind. When seen from the perspective of monotheistic religions such as Christianity and Islam, which concern themselves with the relationship between God and man or the submission of man to an absolute being, Buddhism has features which make it appear quite a different kind of religion altogether.

Buddhism reached China during the Han Dynasty, that is, during the first century A.D., and from the second century onwards Chinese Buddhists applied themselves to the task of translating the scriptures into Chinese. By this means, a Chinese version of Buddhism was created and this, then, spread to the various countries of South-East Asia. The first wave of Buddhism, which consisted of the kind of Buddhism known as the Mahayana or the Great Vehicle, thus spread to Korea and from Korea to Japan, and its emphasis on the pacification and protection of the state was of practical benefit for the rulers and administrators of the states to which it spread.

According to the Japanese chronicles known as *Nihonshoki*, Buddhism is supposed to have first reached Japan in 552 when the King of Paekche presented to the Emperor of Japan a statue of Shakyamuni, some Buddhist scriptures and various other items. There is, however, a strong possibility that well before this date Buddhism was known to individuals in Japan, for at that time there was a considerable amount of human contact between Japan and the Korean peninsula. It seems that at that time there was a tendency for Japanese to think of Buddhism not simply as a religion but as a set of new cultural values. One of the temples dating from this early stage of Japanese Buddhism is the Horyuji, which was constructed at the beginning of the seventh century. The Horyuji was at that time the private possession of the crown prince. In the centre, there was the Golden Hall and a pagoda and behind them a lecture hall, and the whole was surrounded by a gallery which connected up with the main gate at the front. The neat arrangement and the appearance of the buildings were preserved even though they have had to be repaired on numerous occasions, and they remain the world's oldest wooden buildings. The Horyuji still contains a number of Buddhist statues and paintings, religious implements and scriptures dating from the sixth or seventh centuries, and it is to this day a centre of religious activity.

Let us have another look at the Horyuji, placing it in the context of the ordinary village life in the midst of which it stood and about which much can be learnt from archaeological remains and written documents. The area for the temple was set aside in the vicinity of a settlement of houses which had sprung up in the area, and the site for the buildings was carefully laid out with measuring rods. The buildings were covered not with straw or shingles but with tens of thousands of baked tiles. The tall buildings were supported by pillars which were not simply sunk into the ground but were set on stone bases. The pillars were carefully hewn and fitted into a complex wooden framework which enabled a considerable height to be reached. The pillars for the gallery had the curved entasis which is found in Greek architecture and they were painted with cinnabar. Many iron nails were used throughout. The walls were decorated with wall-paintings like those found in the lands to the west of China. The large statues and Buddhist implements inside the buildings were cast in bronze. A large collection of Buddhist scriptures was made, and many written records were kept. These were all elements of a new culture which had not existed in Japan before that time, and the Horyuji represents a concentration of them in one place.

The temples built at that time were, in other words, cultural undertakings which embraced the latest knowledge and technology: the introduction and adoption of Buddhism in Japan did not have all that much to do with religion. The construction of private temples was popular with the larger families as a means of introducing and acquiring the new culture, and one consequence of this was the spread of Buddhism.

In the eighth century the dissemination of Buddhism to the provinces was encouraged as a matter of state policy. This took the form of an order requiring that in each of the provinces a major provincial temple and a convent for nuns be built, and financial help be given to make the construction of the requisite buildings possible. But there was a strong utilitarian motive behind all this, for it was hoped that it would thereby be possible to halt the pestilences and poor harvests which were causing much havoc at the time. In other words, the motive for the construction of these provincial temples did not spring from the desire to spread the Buddhist religion among the populace. This is clear from the fact that the lives of the monks and nuns living in these temples were so strictly regulated as to allow for no contact with the local populace.

The implication of all this is that Buddhism was considered in Japan as little more than a means to various ends, these ends being both administrative and technological. It was only in the Heian period, when Buddhism had assumed a Japanese form, that it first began to spread and develop as a religion in Japan. Even then it continued to be put to political use, but it did not become the basic ideology of national administration. In this respect, its fate in Japan was different from that of Christianity in Europe.

KOYAMA-Shuzo

The Rule of Law in Japan

The Chinese 'Ritsuryo' system, which combined a kind of penal code with an administrative and civil code, provided a common basis of mutual understanding among emerging nations periphery of China.

The Chinese Ritsuryo system was introduced to Japan in the middle of the seventh century. At that time, the Korean peninsula was embroiled in wars that were being conducted in pursuit of national unification: Japan, along with China, attempted to intervene, but the expeditionary force despatched to Korea fared so disastrously that Japan soon found itself in a state of anxiety as it wondered when and if the expected invasion force from the mainland would arrive off the coast of Japan. In Japan, there was therefore an urgent need to dispense with the unstable system of government which had existed hitherto and had largely the character of an alliance with powerful families, and to replace it with a well-organised and powerful state apparatus with centralised powers and the emperor at its head.

In order to achieve this it was decided to take over the Chinese Ritsuryo system wholesale and to base Japanese governmental organisation on it as it was being practiced under the T'ang dynasty in China. By comparison with the social state of affairs holding in Japan at the time, the Ritsuryo system was both highly-developed and unrealistic in that it could not be completely put into operation even in China itself. Thus what the Japanese were seeking to transfer bodily to Japan was an idealized system of administration, and in this respect Japan can be compared with such countries of the New World as the United States and Australia at the times when they were going through the process of national formation. A further point that suggests similarities is the fact that the foreign intellectuals, refugees from the fallen dynasties of China and Korea, had an important part to play in spreading the knowledge of the Ritsuryo system and in seeing to its implementation in Japan.

The first objective under the new system was the creation of a bureaucratic system of government and the establishment of the necessary administrative agencies. The two central agencies established were the Jingikan, which took charge of religious observances, and the Dajokan, which was concerned with general administrative matters and was divided into eight ministries. There were also administrative bodies to supervise the police and oversee military affairs. The total number of the bureaucrats involved may have reached ten thousand.

For provincial administration the entire country was divided up into sixty-one units or provinces, which were further subdivided into counties and villages, each with its own official in charge. The senior administrative official of each province was a member of the central bureaucracy, but members of powerful local families were appointed to undertake the administration of the counties and the villages. The provinces were based on traditional geographical regions and they by and large accord with the provincial government system based on the prefectures that now, some thirteen hundred years later, form the unit of local administration.

The most important task confronting the new administrative system was the strengthening of the financial system of the state. The method used to achieve this was a form of nationalization applied to both the land and the people. National registers were compiled in which was recorded the name, address, age and sex of each person. Paddy fields were laid out on a chessboard pattern with a fixed size, and a fixed piece of public land was allocated to each farmer in accordance with his age and other factors. The farmers were required to pay three per cent of the yield of the fields they had been allotted as a form of tax, and in addition there was a poll tax paid in cloth, silk and salt, and a corvée consisting of sixty days of labour or military service per year. According to documents that have survived, it seems that, at least during the early period, the bureaucracy managed to make a success of the collection of these taxes and to apply them to the running of the country.

But in spite of the supposed 'nationalization' of the people, there was no attempt to treat everybody as equals. The people were divided from the start into the good citizenry and the lowly. The former category included the aristocracy which enjoyed a number of financial and social privileges. The aristocrats were the old powerful families of the Kinai area around Nara and Kyoto, but their status was guaranteed by the fact that under the new system they were granted positions and ranks commensurate with the power they had exercised before the advent of the Ritsuryo system. Under the newly-established system of higher education, their children received education in philosophy, literature, law and arithmetic and they were promised hereditary succession to posts in the bureaucracy. They were exempt from taxes and the corvée and allowed private ownership of their farming land and estates.

The decision to recognize the right of the aristocracy to private ownership of the land, though necessitated by power of the local families in the Kinai area, became in time the cause of the collapse of the Ritsuryo system. Powerful aristocratic families, temples and shrines, strengthened their financial resources by bringing more and more land under cultivation or by receiving donations of land, thereby expanding the territory under their control. The upshot of these developments was the 'Shoen' system of large landed estates. This system has few parallels anywhere in the world: it destroyed the financial basis of the Ritsuryo system leading to the ultimate dissolution of the Risturyo system as an effective form of administration. Nevertheless the bureaucratic apparatus and the laws set up under the Ritsuryo system did exert some influence on the administrative structures of samurai society in later centuries and on common law. Also, many modern legal terms and expressions have their origins in the language of the Ritsuryo system.

In their respective spheres of cultural influence, both the Chinese Ritsuryo system and Roman Law fulfilled roles that are very similar. Roman Law, however, was a system of law detached from social philosophies, while the Ritsuryo system included both law and Confucian philosophical concepts and also had the role of extending the benefits of civilisation. It was probably inevitable, therefore, that the Ritsuryo system would be discarded in the end, for social progress led to growing contradictions between the Ritsuryo system as it existed in theory and the society to which it had been applied.

KOYAMA-Shuzo

1 Nara

It appears from surviving records that until the seventh century a new palace was constructed each time the imperial throne passed to a new incumbent. Fires, rebellions and other disasters also led to the palace being moved to a new site. People at that time apparently believed it possible to escape natural disasters, calamities and misfortune simply by abandoning the old palace for a new one. In the distant past such works of reconstruction were simple affairs, for even the imperial palace then was just part of a village and the administrative organisation was small scale, so only a modest amount of labour was needed to construct the palace and the offices attached to it.

But in time the *ritsuryo* legal system developed in the sixth century A.D. involving both land and people becoming the property of the state and the emerging of a centralized bureaucratic apparatus, as a result of these changes the offices and functions connected with the court grew enormously. This necessitated the establishment of a capital city which could systematically and comfortably accommodate all the offices and functions of the state. The model was of course taken from China. The first such capital, called 'kyō' in Japan, was Fujiwara-kyō, and work was begun on it in 693. As a capital, however, it did not last very long.

Nara (Heijo-kyō) was the first capital of Japan to enjoy a semi-permanent existence. It was in use as the capital from 701 for approximately eighty years and ministered to seven generations of emperors. At the height of its prosperity it was celebrated in poetry and compared to flowers laden with scent and blossom.

The plan of Nara was based on that of Ch'ang-An, the capital of T'ang dynasty in China, so it was oblong in shape with a grid-like structure of streets. At the northern end was the palace and the town was to be found on either side of the main thoroughfare, which stretched from north to south. It measured 4.2 kilometers by 4.6 and so was about one quarter of the size of Ch'ang An. It also differed from its Chinese model in that it was not symmetrical, having an additional part attached to the northeastern corner, and in that it was not surrounded by a city wall.

In addition to the palace, the capital contained the homes of courtiers and the aristocracy, a number of temples, and the markets to the west and east of the main thoroughfare. The total population is reckoned to have been about two hundred thousand.

Towards the end of the period during which Nara was the capital, many plans were made for moving the capital to a new location. In the end the palace was moved to Heian-kyō, present-day Kyoto, and Nara's day came to an end. But the

'Todaiji Daibutsuden' where the great image of Buddha is enshrined

temples of Nara remained and enabled the township to continue in existence. Temples with a history of more than a thousand years, such as the Todaiji, the Kofukuji, the Yakushiji and the Toshodaiji have survived to the twentieth century along with many old Buddhist statues and cultural treasures, and so Nara today is a center of both religious activity and tourism.

Fifty years after the palace had been abandoned for a new one in Kyoto, the site on which it had stood was already nothing more than fields, according to existing contemporary records. For centuries to come its very location was unknown. But in the Edo period the question of its location began to attract attention and studies were pursued with the help of written records. In 1953, however, archaeological excavations enabled the site to be accurately determined, and in 1955 the whole area was made into a park and a special archaeological team was set up to work on the long-term excavation and preservation of the site.

The excavations enabled much to be learnt about the distribution of the buildings within the palace area and the patterns of life of the residents, and other matters which existing documentation threw no light on. In addition to the Administration Hall and the Emperor's Residence Hall, the palace also contained various office buildings for the ten thousand or so officials who thought to have been in the bureaucracy at the time. The excavations revealed the location of these buildings and also made it clear that they had to be rebuilt from time to time as the wooden pillars which formed the framework were sunk straight into the ground, thus shortening the life of the buildings. Many things were found thrown away in the wells and drainage ditches, such as eating implements, tools, writing implements and articles of religious or shamanistic significance. But of greatest interest has been the collection of more than twenty thousand 'mokkan' which has been assembled during the excavations so far. These are pieces of wood with written texts on them and they include official orders and communications, reports, food inventories, work evaluations, documents relating to debts, and even graffiti as well as inventories of items sent from the provinces to Nara as tax in kind. These finds brought to life the daily life of the bureaucrats and their administrative organisation, matters on which it had been impossible to glean anything with the written records that have survived.

Since the excavations were conducted by a nationally funded and supervised body, many advances were made in the techniques of excavation and the preservation of artifacts and structural remains, and Japanese archaeology as a whole, which until then had been conducted on an independent basis by various universities and individuals, saw its level of expertise greatly increased. There is now a national archaeological center which records and reports on archaeological projects throughout Japan and the various archaeological finds, which now exceed six thousand items a year.

KOYAMA-Shuzo

Chinese as a Common Language

The Han Chinese first developed a writing system about four thousand years ago. The Chinese characters that are the components of this writing system are ideographs, each with a meaning of its own, as is evident from the fact that many of them developed from pictographs like the Egyptian hieroglyphics. Written Chinese developed subsequently into an abbreviated form of writing that had a different vocabulary and syntax from those of the spoken language. The earliest examples date from the Yin dynasty (about 1500 to 1000 B.C.) and large numbers of samples of this early form of written Chinese have been found, especially oracular inscriptions on tortoise-shell. These early characters are clearly the ancestors of the Chinese characters used in China and Japan today and there are few of them now that are of uncertain meaning.

Over the subsequent centuries, written Chinese continued to evolve and from about the second century onwards it began to spread from China to the surrounding peoples of East Asia, along with Chinese philosophical ideas such as Confucianism and Chinese technology. Written Chinese came to play a role in East Asia similar to that of Latin in Europe as the language of education for men of good breeding and it became established as the common language of East Asia. In Korea, Viet-Nam, Japan and elsewhere, written Chinese became the official language of state documents. For this reason, although the spoken languages of China and Japan are completely different, even today it is possible to some extent for a Japanese and a Chinese to communicate by means of the written words.

It is thought that the Chinese characters and written Chinese were first introduced to Japan by way of Korea in the fifth century, and many documents written from that time onwards have survived to the present day. But the linguistic structures of Japanese and Chinese are quite different. Accordingly, passages of written Chinese needed to be adapted in some way if they were to be comprehensible to Japanese. The method developed was one that involved first of all accepting Chinese lexical items as loan words and adapting their pronunciation to suit the Japanese phonological system; numerical signs and symbols were used to convert the word order of the original Chinese into that of Japanese, and particles and other linguistic elements needed in Japanese, but not in Chinese, were added to the text. This method of reading Chinese as if it were Japanese was made official in Japan about the tenth century and in the course of time it came to be widely used.

As a consequence, written Chinese inevitably had a great influence on the Japanese language. Just as Greek and Latin are used in the languages of Europe to create new words or technical vocabulary, so in Japan, Chinese is used for similar purposes. Some of these Chinese-type words coined in Japan have been exported to China, where many of them are now in wide use. Another area of Chinese influence was visible in the emergence of a style of written Japanese that relied heavily on Chinese manners of expression.

Over the centuries an enormous number of books written in Chinese have been brought to

Japan, but the sorts of Chinese written by Japanese have varied from age to age. From the early period there had survived a number of funereal inscriptions and inlaid inscriptions in iron swords, but in the eighth century various books were compiled in Chinese such as *Kojiki* (Record of Ancient Matters), *Nihonshoki* (Chronicles of Japan), *Fudoki* or economic and geographic reports compiled by local administrative authorities in the provinces, collections of Chinese poetry and so on. During these early years many migrants from the continent had chosen to settle in Japan and there were also many Japanese who had received some of their education in China as members of official missions to the T'ang court, so Chinese written by Japanese was of a comparatively high standard. But in the tenth century, around the middle of the Heian period, relations between Japan and China came to an end with the collapse of the T'ang dynasty: thereafter the quality of Chinese written by Japanese deteriorated.

During the Kamakura period (1185-1333), when the samurai came to the fore, the Zen sect of Buddhism which enjoyed the patronage and support of many samurai, sent priests to China for study and also invited Chinese priests to teach in Japan. Through these contacts between China and Japan the new styles of written Chinese that had developed during the Chinese Sung dynasty reached Japan. This led to the so-called 'Five Mountains' Zen literature which was founded on these new styles of written Chinese. Among the samurai, however, education in Chinese composition did not spread to any great extent and so it was rather Japanese styles of written Chinese that came to be more commonly practised.

During the Edo period (1600-1868), Confucianism became the official ideology and the bakufu government established an academy and a shrine in honour of Confucius in Edo. Following the example set by bakufu, all the han appointed their own Confucian teachers and han schools, and education in written Chinese based on the classical texts of Confucianism came to be conducted on a national scale. At the extreme end of the process were the 'terakoya' schools where the commoners acquired a similar sort of education. Thus most Japanese during the Edo period had some contact at least with written Chinese.

Since Japan is an island country and has enjoyed few opportunities for direct contacts with other peoples, new ideas and new technologies have usually been introduced to Japan through the medium of the written words. From the fifth century right up to the time when Japan began to look to European books to acquire the elements of modern technology, that role was played by written Chinese. So for the acquisition and absorption of information, a knowledge of the language in which it was written was essential, but there was no great need to be able to write in a foreign language in order to transmit information. In Japan today there are many people who say that they cannot speak English, but most of them have a good command of written English and can read it with ease. This probably has a lot to do with the kind of attitudes towards foreign languages that developed during Japan's long association with written Chinese.

KOYAMA-Shuzo

｜The Language the Japanese Speak

The Japanese language is used virtually no-where outside Japan, and it is sometimes said to be related to no other language in the world. In the area around Japan there are such languages as Korean, which is similarly remote from other languages, Tungusic, Mongolian and the other Altaic languages on the north of the Asiatic mainland, and to the south there is Chinese and the other languages of the Sino-Tibetan family. And in the South Pacific region there are the Malayo-Polynesian languages. But none of these languages has a close relationship with Japanese that can be demonstrated by linguistically acceptable evidence.

Within Japan the Ryukyuan and Ainu languages are also to be found. Ryukyuan has a number of close phonetic correspondences with Japanese and it is very closely related to Japanese: the two are thought to have separated between two thousand and one thousand five hundred years ago. Ainu, on the other hand, is very different from Japanese and its linguistic relationship with other languages has been unclear for a long time. Recent research, however, has revealed that its structural features closely resemble those of Japanese and, when consideration is given to the results of archaeological and anthropological research, it would appear that Ainu separated from Japanese at a very early stage, well before 200 B.C.. There are many Ainu place-names in Hokkaido today, and many place-names survive in northern Honshu, too, that are thought to be of Ainu origins.

Japan has for a long time had close cultural links with the Korean peninsula and the Korean language exhibits a word order and grammar that are more or less identical to those of Japan. There are other features that the two languages have in common too, such as vowel harmony and the lack of any words beginning with r or l, but in spite of these similarities, there are few lexical correspondences and so no proof that they belong to the same language group. If they do in fact belong to the same language group, then they would have to have drawn apart from common roots about five thousand years ago, according to the method of determining the relative age of languages known as glottochronology. Accordingly, if Japanese is related to Mongolian, Tungusic and the other Altaic languages, it would have to have separated from them much earlier still.

There are also some scholars who argue for a close relationship between Japanese and the Austronesian languages of the South Pacific. Their arguments are largely based on the facts that these languages have simple consonant systems and a tendency for words to end in a vowel, like Japanese, but there is little correspondence in matters of grammar and phonology. One suggestion that has been put forward is that the ancestor of the Japanese language evolved out of a meeting between an Altaic language and an Austronesian language on the Korean peninsula and that it then moved into western Japan where it again came into contact with an Austronesian language. Other scholars have suggested a relationship between Japanese and Papuan, pointing out that the grammar, phonology and word order of the two languages are close and that basic lexical

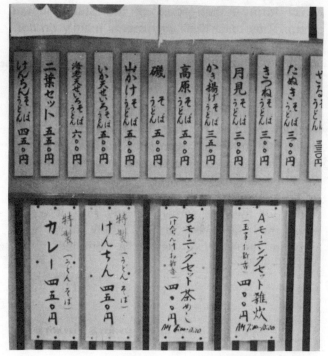

Menu item on restaurant wall

items exhibit more correspondence than they do in the case of the Altaic languages and Japanese.

The Sino-Tibetan language group dominates the central and southern parts of East Asia, but Japanese is usually considered to have no linguistic connection with Chinese. The influence of Chinese, however, has been great. Since Chinese characters have now been in use in Japan for many centuries, Japanese contains many Chinese loan words—about forty per cent of words now used in Japanese originally came from Chinese. So, as neighbours the two languages have come to have a lot in common. Some scholars have also suggested a linguistic connection between Japanese and the Tibeto-Burmese languages, which form a sub-group of the Shino-Tibetan group. They base their arguments mainly on correspondences in the formation of lexical roots and personal pronouns.

The likelihood is that an ancestor of the modern Japanese language was in existence by the Jomon period (up to 200 B.C.) and that it developed into the modern language over a long period during which elements from a variety of other languages were absorbed and the influence of other languages was felt. Such a process would explain why so many different theories are being put forward today. At any rate, it would seem that Japanese is like many other phenomena in Japan in having a complex, multi-layered character.

KOYAMA-Shuzo

And How They Write

The Chinese characters were the first writing system to be used in Japan. It is recorded in *Kojiki* (Record of Ancient Matters) that the characters were introduced to Japan when *Thousand Character Classic* and *Analects of Confucius* were brought to Japan from Paekche in Korea. However, a number of swords, mirrors and other funerary objects found in burial mounds in Japan have had Chinese characters inscribed on them, so it is apparent that they had come into use at an earlier date than that mentioned in the official records.

The characters were developed for writing Chinese, and were quite unsuitable for writing Japanese, which is structurally a completely different kind of language. The characters are basically ideographs—each one having a meaning of its own—but in Japan the method that was first adopted involved using them for their pronunciations to represent Japanese sounds, irrespective of their meanings. Even today this method of using the characters is still used in China for writing loan words and names from English and other languages.

All the four thousand five hundred or so poems in *Manyōshu* (Anthology of Ten Thousand Leaves), an anthology compiled in the eighth century, are written in a manner developed indigenously in Japan. This manner of writing Japanese by means of Chinese characters is known as 'Manyōgana', from the anthology in which it was first used. In the 'Manyōgana' system, the characters were used methodically, with particular characters being used to represent particular sounds in Japanese. By carefully comparing the use of characters in the *Manyōshu* with the pronunciation of those characters in the Chinese of that time, it has been possible for linguists to ascertain that the ancient Japanese language had eighty-eight sounds and was thus phonetically more diverse and more complex than the modern Japanese language.

However, 'Manyōgana' were cumbersome, for the system made use of many different Chinese characters each of which was complex and required many strokes of the brush. To cope with these problems a simpler phonetic system was developed by Japanese for use in Japan, consisting of two syllabaries known as the katakana and the hiragana.

The katakana consist of highly simplified signs formed by taking just one part of an original Chinese character. They developed in Buddhist institutions for the purpose of making annotations in sutras so that they would be easier to read. Subsequently, however, the katakana signs came to be used for documents in which they appeared side by side with Chinese characters, and here their function was to represent the inflections and particles of Japanese, which have no equivalent in Chinese.

The hiragana are signs formed by reducing the original character to a simplifed representation not of one part but of the overall shape of the character. These signs were called 'women's letters', for they were widely used by the aristocratic women of the Heian Period (794-1185) in diaries and letters, while men used pure Chinese written only in characters for their official documents. But in the social world of the period, the exchange of love-letters was a normal part of life, so that men too had to know the hiragana. It occasionally happened that a male poet took a feminine pen-name and wrote a poetic diary in hiragana.

Until about the tenth century, the katakana signs showed a lot of variation, for there were different schools of usage as well as personal idiosyncrasies. They were gradually brought into some kind of order, and the forms in which they are used today were more or less fixed by the fifteenth century. The hiragana signs, on the other hand, had been developed with practical purposes in mind and so there were few original signs. But a certain snobbism emerged in time as a response to the spread and popularization of the hiragana, and this took the form of introducing variant forms for their own sake. But at least this development did add to the complex beauty of Japanese calligraphy.

In 1900 the Japanese government officially designated the hiragana and katakana as the scripts of Japan and the forms they have now were fixed in that year. Contemporary Japanese is written using these two kana syllabaries and about two thousand Chinese characters. Recently many words from English and other languages have been introduced into the Japanese language and it is not uncommon to find words written in the roman alphabet in the middle of the passages of Japanese writing. It thus takes a considerable amount of time to learn how to read and write Japanese, and especially to master the Chinese characters, and as a result much time is devoted to these tasks during the nine years of compulsory eduction in Japan.

It will be clear from the above that the printing of Japanese requires a lot of time and skill, involving as it does the selection one by one of letters and characters of different kinds. Nevertheless, printing and publishing are flourishing industries in Japan and such newspapers as the Yomiuri, with a circulation of 8,740,000, the Asahi, with a circulation of 7,470,000 and the Mainichi, with a circulation of 4,540,000, are among the world's best-selling newspapers, alongside Pravda from the Soviet Union (over ten million copies), Renmin Erbao from the People's Republic of China (seven million copies), and Die Welt from West Germany (nearly six million copies).

As for books, there are more than three thousand publishing companies in Japan. They produce more than thirty thousand new titles each year, and a total of thirty thousand million copies of books altogether. In addition, more than three thousand million copies of magazines are published each year.

Japanese printing is now in the process of going through an electronic revolution. Japanese word processors are now on the market - they are known as wâpuro in Japan—from an abbreviation of wâdo-purosessâ (= word processor in Japanese pronunciation). The input can take the form of kana or roman letters and the computer memory can convert them into characters at the push of a button. As word processors become smaller in size and cheaper to purchase, they are approaching the functions and convenience of the typewriter for alphabetic languages like English. It seems likely that in the future, documents and letters which have long been written out by hand in Japan will be printed by word processors.

KOYAMA-Shuzo

Poems and Novels

In Japan there are two traditional poetic forms that are both extremely short: the tanka and the haiku. Because the majority of words in the Japanese language end in one of the five vowels, although rhyme is very simple to achieve, the result tends to be somewhat monotonous. For this reason the Japanese have developed a form of verse in which syllable count is employed rather than rhyme. For instance, the tanka consists of five lines with 5, 7, 5, 7 and 7 syllables, respectively. The haiku is in effect an abbreviated form of the tanka, in which the first three lines - with 5, 7 and 5 syllables - are retained, minus the final 14 syllables. The former has a very long history, being one of the first poetic forms to be recorded in Japan. The haiku, on the other hand, is more recent, having developed from the tanka in the sixteenth century to become an independent verse form.

The first poetic anthology to appear in Japan was *Manyōshu* (Anthology of Ten Thousand Leaves), compiled in the eighth century. It contains approximately 4,500 poems and songs composed by the ancient Japanese, the vast majority of which are tanka. These poems can be roughly divided into three groups: banka, or elegies; sōmonka, or epistolary poems often concerned with love themes; and the miscellaneous zōka. A finer classification reveals such sub-categories as duologues, travel poems, poems of the four seasons, poems of parting, and the so-called azuma-uta, or 'Eastland Poems' originating in the eastern Azuma region of Japan. Reading these, one can appreciate how the people of the time tried to express various emotions and describe various scenes in the restricted poetic format of only 31 syllables. It is not surprising, therefore, that the diction tends to be extremely terse, while symbolism and allusions abound. Thus it is that poems of the senses, rather than of the intellect, preponderate. The poet avoids limiting the meaning of a particular word or using precise expressions, and purposely gives his phrases a very amorphous, wide-ranging semantic domain which enables many different interpretations. Such a technique makes full use of one of the special characteristics of the Japanese language: its ambiguity.

Contributors to *Manyōshu* anthology include people from all stations of life, from emperors and aristocrats, to farmers and fishers, prostitutes and beggars. Although many of these were amateurs, professional poets are also in evidence.

After the obvious popularity it enjoyed in the eighth century, the tanka was temporarily eclipsed by Chinese verse (as composed by the Japanese). However, before long the tanka made a comeback thanks mainly to the development of the kana syllabary which greatly facilitated the recording of the spoken language on paper (previously Chinese characters had been used). The kana script was mostly favored by the ladies at court, and it was in these circles that the tanka made its revival. The court also became the venue for frequent competitions at which teams of poets vied to outdo each other in composing verse, and poems were often solicited to celebrate certain important occasions. A major event in the history of tanka occurred in the beginning of the tenth century when the emperor commissioned what was to be the first imperial anthology of Japanese verse. Over the following five hundred years a total of 21 such imperial anthologies were compiled. Tanka thus became one of the major artistic forms in Japan, its popularity spreading once more through the populace, from the aristocrats to the warriors, and from them to the merchants.

The tanka is still alive and well in modern Japan. Every year the emperor decides on a theme such as 'islands', 'lanterns' or 'greenery' on which tanka are to be composed for the New Year Poetry Party. The competition is open to all, and in 1983 as many as 26,570 poems were received, of which the best ten were selected. The successful entrants included a housewife, a businessman, a teacher and a carpenter. Since it was first recorded in the eighth century, the tanka has maintained exactly the same format (although the position of the caesura has changed), and the diction employed has altered but little. As a literary form it has thus displayed remarkable continuity. Furthermore, it has been popular with a wide spectrum of the population.

Japanese literature comprises more than just poetry, of course; there is a wealth of prose, but perhaps the best example is the work *Genji monogatari,* or 'The Tale of Genji'. It is thought to have been written by a lady who served at court at the beginning of the eleventh century. 'The Tale of Genji' is a lengthy romance which revolves around the life of a very handsome, noble prince called the 'Shining Genji' - and especially around his relationships with various women. In the ancient literatures of India and Europe one finds epic poems in which are related the superhuman exploits or crushing tragedies of a nobleman or a saint, as well as stories involving mere tender subjects. But 'The Tale of Genji' is quite different. There are no spectacular events, only glimpses of the ordinary, albeit aristocratic, life and thoughts of a human being; it is, in a way, a type of psychological novel. And, despite being one of the longest novels in the world, this 54-chapter romance has a distinctive serial nature.

In Japanese literature there is often a compelling interest in the everyday, almost trivial aspects of life. Thus there are countless diaries, travel accounts and pensées of various kinds. An important prose genre comprises the so-called 'I' novels which contain nothing more than the details of the author's own life and thoughts, as well as those of his/her close friends and relations.

Sustained narratives were, however, written around the thirteenth century in the form of numerous war tales, but most narratives were either direct translations or adaptations of foreign works; up until the middle of the nineteenth century these were mainly Chinese, but since then European literature has furnished much raw material. In fact, in Japan, translations are considered to form a literary genre of their own, and important modern works from such countries as China, Russia, Britain, France, Germany and the Scandinavian states have virtually all been published in Japanese. Recent statistics show that nearly 600 books – from various countries of the world – are translated and published each year, proving that the profession of the translator is solidly established in Japan.

KOYAMA-Shuzo

Shinto

When Japanese were asked in a recent survey what religion they believed in, twenty-seven per cent said Buddhism, just over three per cent said Shinto, one per cent said Christianity, and sixty-five per cent or so said that they had no religion at all. It would appear from the results of this survey that the Japanese are not very interested in religion and in particular that there are very few who believe in Shinto, Japan's own ancient religion.

Matters are much less clear, however, when statistics of a different kind are considered, such as the numbers of people paying New Year visits to Shinto shrines. It seems that throughout the country more than seventy-eight million people

Yushima Tenjin Shrine in Tokyo

visit shrines, and this figure includes the more than three million who visit the Meiji Shrine in Tokyo. Futhermore, no traditional town or village is without a shrine in honour of its tutelary deity where large festivals are held every year in spring and autumn. Shinto continues to have a place in everyday life too, for many people attach protective Shinto amulets to their motorcars; it is common to hold ground-breaking ceremonies on sites where bridges or buildings are to be constructed; and there are often small Shinto shrines on the tops of modern office buildings. Also, in the home it is usual to have a kamidana, a shelf for the household gods, as well as a small Buddhist altar. So in spite of the surveys, it seems that the attachment of the Japanese people to Shinto is still strong. However, the forms that faith and practice take in Shinto are quite different from those that they take, for example, in the case of a monotheistic religion like Christianity.

Shinto is basically an animistic religion that perceives the presence of gods or of the sacred in animals, in plants, and even in things which have no life, such as stones and waterfalls. The roots go back to the distant past. A large number of items discovered amongst remains dating from the Jōmon period (up to 200 B.C.) are thought to have had some magical significance, for example figures made of stone or clay, stones shaped like mushrooms, and stone circles. Also, many finds have been made of collections of votive gifts dating from the earliest times and consisting of models of mirrors, jewels, houses and human beings, fashioned out of stone or clay. In most cases the finds are made at sites closely connected with Shinto shrines today, such as rocks or mountains with unusual shapes, ponds and wells, islands at strategic or dangerous points on sailing routes, and so on. When the remains of houses are excavated too, it is common to find such votive offerings in the area occupied by the kitchen.

Shinto would thus appear to be a Japanese form of religious practice which enjoys close ties with people's everyday lives, and which did so in the past too. It does not seem to have had the form of an organized or systematized religion. Indeed, Shinto only became a systematized religion when it was faced with the competition of the newly-imported religion, Buddhism.

According to the historical chronicles, Buddhism reached Japan in either 538 or 552. At first it seems to have been seen not so much as a religion but as simply a new form of knowledge, which was monopolized by particular groups in Japanese society, such as the immigrants and aristocrats who were endeavouring to import the civilization of mainland China to Japan. But as time passed, understanding of the new religion increased among the aristocrats and intellectuals gathering around the court, and some people had sufficient faith to take the tonsure. Eventually there were attempts to make it the national religion of Japan, and a number of emperors became believers in Buddhism.

But in Japanese society the emperor's role in both theory and practice was to conduct Shinto rituals as well as affairs of state. So a religion like Buddhism which stressed the idea of the transmigration of souls and the existence of an absolute being who was superior to the emperor threatened to negate the very foundations of the Japanese state. For this reason it was necessary for the supporters of Buddhism to show that Buddhism could be of benefit to the state, and for this purpose it was very convenient that early Japanese Buddhism was of the Mahayana variety, which is more solicitous for the welfare of the state than other varieties.

Meanwhile those on the side of Shinto were striving to turn it from the primitive religion it had long been into a religion with a philosophy and a structure that would enable it to compete with Buddhism. This was the beginning of the transformation of Shinto into a state religion, and it meant that Buddhism and Shinto did not so much combine as remain two parallel religions in Japan. Thus during the Edo period, almost all Japanese had some contacts with Buddhism, for the Buddhist temples had responsibility for conducting burial rites, whereas Shinto remained the religion of the daily lives to most people.

The phenomenon of a highly systematized and organised religion overlaying but not replacing a primitive religion can also be found in the history of the spread of Christianity and Islam too. But even without looking at the examples provided by the Roman and Saracen empires, there are many cases where rulers of a new religion take over from rulers of an old religion, and as the new religion spreads among the people, the old one is gradually pushed into the background and suppressed, to survive only as a few fragmentary practice taken up into the new religion. The coexistence of Buddhism and Shinto provides quite a contrast with such cases as these.

KOYAMA-Shuzo

˺ The Web of Ancient Myths

In the eighth century two historical chronicles were compiled in Japan, one called the *Kojiki* (Record of Ancient matters) and the other the *Nihon shoki* (Chronicles of Japan). The *Nihon shoki* was put together in 720 as an official history of the Japanese state and its thirty books covers the time from the creation of the heavens and the earth up to the time of the supposed forty-first sovereign of Japan, the Empress Jitō. The events of each reign are recorded in chronological order. The sections which cover the age of the gods and the years of the early emperors are based not on historical fact, of course, but constitute a pseudo-history consisting of myths and legends arranged within a historical framework. It is considered that the compilers of these early sections were seeking to demonstrate that Japan was an old country with a noble history, and that its sovereigns, the emperors and empresses, were the only legitimate rulers of the lands. There are elements here of an intense nationalism that contained a determination to assert Japan's independence from China as a country in her own right on a par with China.

The myths written down in the *Kojiki* and the *Nihon shoki* do not constitute a unified and consistent whole. Rather, many different versions are recorded with elements and plots that are sometimes widely divergent. A comparison of these myths and their various versions with the myths of other peoples in the world reveals that the Japanese myths are strongly tied to particular areas, as will be clear from what follows.

In the first place, it is apparent that the

Japanese myths and those of the southern Pacific region have many points in common. According to the Japanese myths, before the creation of the heavens and the earth, there was a world of emptiness and chaos, and it was here that the gods first appeared. Gods continued to appear from then on, reflecting the gradual development of the universe; finally a god and a goddess were born who came down to earth, married and gave birth to land and man; and they raised up islands from the sea bed which became the islands of Japan. There are many similarities between this story and the myths that are found in the islands of Polynesia. Other Japanese myths are similar to myths found in the South Pacific, Indonesia and New Guinea, and one of them is the myth that tells how plants for cultivation first appeared on various parts of the body of a goddess who had been killed. Another is the story of the man who borrowed a fishhook and went fishing; he lost the hook and when pressed hard to return it by the man who had lent it to him, he went as far as the bottom of the sea in search of it; he found it stuck in the throat of a fish, so he was able to return it and thus get his own back on the man who had insisted on its return.

There are many points in common between the myths of South East Asia, including Japan, and the Pacific Region. But whereas the plants issuing from the body of the goddess are coconut palms and banana trees in the South Pacific, in South-East Asia they are plants more familiar to the peoples of the area, such as rice, millet, red beans, barley and soya beans. And in the South-East Asian versions, the man who goes down to the bottom of the sea in search of a fish hook marries a dragon woman and they have children;

and the first ancestors of the race produce a deformed child (in many cases the marriage is between a brother and sister, so there appears to be an indication of an incest taboo here). Thus there are in the South-East Asian myths elements that differ from those of the South Pacific, and what is more the plots of the myths develop in different ways.

Also in South-East Asia there is a unique myth explaining the phenomenon of the eclipse of the sun. The sun, a goddess, goes into hiding and the world is plunged into darkness and confusion, but she is tricked into showing herself again by the cackling of some hens and a kind of strip-tease dance.

One of the most interesting results of recent studies in comparative mythology has been the suggestion that there are areas of similarity between the myths of Japan and those of Greece. In Japan the God Izanagi, who wants to bring back his wife who has died in childbirth, braves the dangers of going down to the underworld in search of her. But he finds it impossible to bring her back because she had already eaten the food of the realm of the dead and because he has disobeyed the prohibition on looking at her corpse. This story is very similar to that of Orpheus in Greek mythology. There are many cases in the world where myths from different countries are similar, but the only case involving similarity in both plot outline and in details is this one connecting Japan and Greece, excepting only the case of the mythological traditions of the North American Indians.

It is possible to see in these similarities between Japanese myths and those of other areas evidence of various cultural impacts on Japan at various times. Thus the similarities with the Pacific Region would appear to be closely connected with the Stone Age culture of earliest times when the cultivation of the taro and the art to fishing reached Japan after travelling along the route followed by the Kuro Shio current, passing from island to island. The similarities with South-East Asia are probably connected with introduction of rice cultivation to Japan and, before that, with the introduction of the cultivation of various other cereals. And the myths that are similar to those of Greece were probably brought to Japan by such horse-riding peoples of northern Eurasia as the Tungusic tribes.

It has been suggested that, some time around the fourth or fifth centuries, these horse-riding peoples crossed the sea and conquered Japan, which was then just in the process of forming a unified state, and that they took the place of the old ruling class of Japan. This theory is supported by the similarity between the myths of Japan and ancient Greece and by the supposition that these myths were brought to Japan by the horse-riding peoples of northern Eurasia. But it is not only Japan's myths that are multi-layered in this way, for the same applies to its language and much of its material culture as well.

KOYAMA-Shuzo

The Samurai

The samurai were men who specialised in arms and warfare and thus equivalent to the knights of Europe.

The samurai came into existence around the time in the ninth century when the 'Ritsuryo' system of government, which had been established in Japan in the seventh century, was facing a crisis and new forces were emerging in the provinces. As local administration in the provinces weakened and grew more chaotic, powerful local families armed themselves and, relying on their new strength, refused to pay the tax-demands presented to them by the administrative officials who were sent out by the central government. These officials in their turn set about equipping themselves militarily, too, so as to be able to defend themselves, and some of them even chose to remain in the provinces after the expiry of their terms of office and to become powerful local families in their own right. It was these people in the provinces, armed for offensive or defensive reasons, that gradually developed into the warriors known today as the samurai.

From about the eleventh century, these samurai who had acquired their strength in the provinces began to move closer and closer to the capital. They were mostly hired for their military strength and were used to protect the persons and property of the senior members of the aristocracy. They were called 'samurai' by the people of the time: the word is a substantival form of the verb 'saburau' and it used to refer to people who were in close attendance on their master or lord. At first their social position was extremely low, as the meaning of the word indicates. Meanwhile, samurai in the provinces were constantly rebelling against central authority and other samurai were playing an important role in putting down these rebellions. This state of affairs gradually brought home to people the relative weakness of the aristocrats in the capital and drew attention to the flow of power from them to the samurai and the provinces. Finally at the end of the twelfth century Minamoto Yoritomo, the foremost among the samurai at that time, established a new government in Kamakura near modern Tokyo. This new government was composed of samurai and heralded the start of the Kamakura period in Japanese history.

The emergence and growth of the samurai as a class owes much to their coming together in groups for self-defence, and these groups became characterized by the development of lord-vassal relationships. Minamoto Yoritomo gave the samurai who had constituted his band of followers nominal positions as provincial administrators and thereby gave them territory and an income. This was regarded as a mark of his favour to his followers. They in their turn were required to submit to his orders even at the cost of their lives on the outbreak of war, and in times of peace to guard and protect him in rotation. This was the service they rendered to him. The relationship between lord and vassal, which was marked by the combination of favour and service, is very similar to that between the sovereign and knights of medieval Europe. In Europe, the relationship based on protection and loyalty formed a kind of mutual contract: the duties of the knights were stipulated and they even had the right to appeal. In Japan, the samurai enjoyed a similar kind of

mutual contract.

Some mention should be made here of bushido, the code of ethics which the bushi or samurai were bound to obey. Naturally, they were first and foremost expected to show bravery in the face of the enemy even if their own lives were at risk. But there was also awareness of the need for peace to be preserved under the new government, and so unruly the conduct was outlawed and decorum highly regarded. Also, samurai were required to attach importance not only to their own honour and that of their comrades but even that of their enemies. Thus, the bushido of the samurai had such points as the pride, mercy, service and courtesy valued also by the knight of Europe.

So under a government composed of the samurai, Japan developed into a kind of feudal society. As military specialists, samurai occupied now the highest position in society, like the knights of Europe. They were tied to each other in vertical relationships expressed by the concepts of favour and service and they received land from their masters.

When one turns one's attention to East Asia, what is immediately striking is that no other country developed into a feudal society like Japan. In the seventh century Japan had modelled its government on the Chinese system and had established an early state with concentrated powers. There was no precedent in China for the progress from early statehood to a new model of statehood based on feudalism, so Japan had to find its own way. If a society could not find its own way out of a pattern of statehood which was becoming increasingly difficult to maintain and could not find a new pattern, it would cease to develop and would fossilize, like ancient Egypt. Of all the countries of Asia, including China, that were seeking to break out of the mould, Japan alone was successful in achieving the transition to a medieval state, and this is a fact of great significance in world history. There is a parallel between the way in which Japan diverged from China and set on its own path and the way in which the Germanic tribes won independence from the Latin world and formed the medieval European world. The processes of historical development here are similar. Thus the age opened up by the samurai was one which marked a major turning point in Japan's history.

TANI-Naoki

Records and Archives

The oldest surviving documents in Japan are household registers that were compiled in 702 A.D.. Each century from the eighth to the nineteenth has left documents and records of all sorts in enormous quantities, and in terms of their age and quantity Japan may be able to claim to lead the world. At any rate, it is no exaggeration to say that the abundance of documentary materials has provided a great stimulus to historical research in Japan.

Under the 'Ritsuryo' system, the centralized form of government taken over from China, the notion of records was one that only encompassed official records. But after the collapse of the 'Ritsuryo' system and the spread of the private ownership of land, powerful country families began to keep their own records, and these were the first private records that had been kept in Japan. After the turn of the millenium, documents and records became indispensable for asserting rights to plots of land and property, whether it was a manorial estate or a domestic plot of land that was at stake.

Under the samurai government of the Middle Ages, the expressions 'issho-kenmei' and 'ando' became popular. The first of these, in the meaning of 'great effort' or 'determination', is still widely used today, but the word 'kenmei' that forms the second half this expression has that meaning on its own. The first half of the expression, 'issho', means '(one) place', and the combination of the two words yielded the meaning of being determined to protect a piece of land, namely the territory of a samurai. The second word, 'ando', on the other hand, is used now in the sense of 'peace of mind' or 'reassurance', but it originally signified the public recognition of ownership rights to a piece of land. Together, then, these two expressions indicated the samurai's determination to protect the land that was the source of his livelihood, and the peace of mind derived from the document given him by his lord in confirmation of his ownership rights.

There is one other kind of document relating to land that I would like to mention here. From the Middle Ages onwards it was the rule that, when the rights pertaining to a piece of land passed to someone else, letters of proof were exchanged by the seller and the purchaser together with all the documents relating to that piece of land hitherto. In many cases therefore some dozens of documents were involved in the transfer of property rights. In the case of some plots of land in Kyoto, it is possible to name the owners for generation after generation, even as far back as the tenth century. There is possibly no city in the world that can rival Kyoto in this respect.

The attachment to land ownership evidenced by these documents, however, also led to various kinds of dispute. Accordingly in 1232 the first samurai code of law was drawn up. The constituent articles were based on principles of Chinese political philosophy and they determined the rights and obligations of the samurai and the regulations for inheritance and succession. They also laid down the principle of an impartial hearing in a court of law. Thus the establishment of the rule of law in Japan dates back to the thirteenth century. Now that courts of law had been established it became necessary to develop techniques to determine whether documents submitted in evidence were genuine or not. Similar developments took place in Mediaeval Europe occasioned by the need to ascertain the authenticity of documents submitted as legal evidence. In Japan, it did not take very long for the concept of the rule of law to spread to the rural population and the ordinary townspeople. By the fourteenth century villages throughout Japan were beginning to resort to legal processes in order to gain the reversion of lands that had formerly been under their control. They kept their own records of these court cases and it is not unusual for a case of this kind involving a single village to have produced more than a thousand related documents.

It is clear that Mediaeval Japanese society was at all levels concerned with land ownership and with documentary evidence guaranteeing that ownership. It was considered important to keep documents readily available so that they could be checked at any time, so the greatest care was

Old warehouse of Ito family in Ōshima country, Yamaguchi prefecture

given to their preservation and protection. In towns they were kept in the town meeting place, in villages at the local tutelary shrine, and temples and shrines had their own repositories too. So whereas in Mediaeval Europe churches and monasteries were used as archival repositiories and later feudal lords built their own archival repositories for the public preservation of documents, in Japan documents and records were passed from generation to generation privately and unofficially. If there were a fire and it was impossible to remove the documents to a safe place, they would often be thrown into a well, still in their boxes, and rescued once the fire had died down. Since Japanese hand-made papers are strong, they were easily able to withstand being soaked and then dried out, with very little damage. It is thanks to measures such as these that so many documents have survived to the present day.

It is well known that Mediaeval Europe was a society that depended in various ways on documentation of all sorts, and, like Japan, large numbers of documents have survived in both England and France. But the situation is different in Japan's continental neighbor, China. China's history is one of a succession of strong centralized governmental systems rising and falling one after the other. Not only were there no private documents in China, but it was even rare for people to write books in a private capacity, for there was a strong sense that books were the domain of officialdom. By contrast, the survival of documents in Europe and Japan testifies to the prominent role played in those countries by people who had no official position.

TANI-Naoki

꒩Castles

Castles are structures for protecting family and property from the enemy, so their planning has always required a great deal of knowledge and skill. Although Japan and Europe are far removed from each other, it is surprising how much their castles have in common. Thus a comparison of their defensive facilities reveals that they are alike in surrounding the central castle with many rings of moats and walls and in erecting towers at strategic points.

Let us look at some examples: In Europe some castles may be planned so that the attacking forces have to expose the right sides of their bodies as they approach the entrance. The reason for this is that soldiers carried their shields on their left arms and their swords in their right hands, thus leaving their right sides with little defence against arrows or gunfire from the castle. In Japan soldiers carried no shields, but they held bows and guns in their left hands and used both hands to fire with, so castles were made with twists and turns at the entrance forcing the attacking forces to expose themselves to the onslaught of the defenders. Thus in both the West and the East the same fundamental principle was at work guiding the planning and construction of castles.

But there are also differences between the castles of Japan and those of Europe. One of these concerns the consideration given to the possible attack by cannon fire. It is worth noting here that Rutherford Alcock, who came to Japan in the nineteenth century and was the first British diplomatic representative in Japan, pointed out that the arrangement of ramparts and moats and so on in Japanese castles looked strong and easy to defend, but that very little thought had been given to any of the architectural features which were essential if a castle was to be able to withstand bombardment.

A second difference relates to the surrounding castle-towns. In Europe the castle-town was sometimes included within the walls of the castle, and there the merchants and artisans and occasionally even the peasants lived. The same was true of Chinese castles too, with the whole town being contained within the castle walls which were also the city boundaries. But in Japan, the castle-towns grew up only outside the castle walls and were quite undefended. In time of war, the townships were set on fire by the attacking forces, or were even set on fire by the defenders themselves to prevent the enemy deriving any advantage from the presence of a town to plunder. Unlike the inhabitants of a free city like Sakai near Osaka, the inhabitants of Japanese castle-towns had no sense of solidarity or of the need to defend themselves. This is one of the peculiarities of Japanese castle-towns.

Many early Japanese castles were set on hills or mountains. This made it possible to make skillful use of the surrounding terrain in planning for the defence of the castle, and the prime consideration was clearly a strategic one. In the second half of the sixteenth century, however, castles had also come to take on the role of a point from which a whole province or territory was ruled and overseen and their locations shifted from mountains to the plains. Now castles had both political and military significance. The prime symbol of the political element was the development of the tenshukaku or donjon, which rapidly became a feature that combined impressiveness with beauty. The tenshukaku was a lofty structure consisting of between three and seven storeys corresponding to the keep in European castles. The earliest tenshukaku in Japan, and one which deserves attention in connection with European castle architecture, is the one of Azuchi castle, which was completed in the year 1579. Azuchi was the castle of Oda Nobunaga, who brought peace and unification to the country after winning the wars that had wracked Japan during the sixteenth century and who had risen to be the de facto ruler of Japan. According to the results of recent research, the tenshukaku of this castle appeared to have five storeys to the person viewing it from the outside but actually had one underground storey and a total of six storeys above ground, and a height of some forty-six metres, including the stone ramparts surrounding it. The top storey had a room of gold decorated with pictures inspired by Chinese Confucianism, while the fifth floor was decorated in a Buddhist style. On the ground floor there was a tower symbolizing Buddhism which reached up through the ceilings to the third floor. This arrangement is in some ways similar to that found in some large halls in some European castles and since it is unique in Japan it is possible that there may have been some European influence at work here. The construction of tenshukaku began with that at Azuchi castle but in the early part of the seventeenth century tenshukaku were constructed in other parts of the country. When one looks at the beautiful structure of the tenshukaku of Himeji castle, which is often compared to a white crane in appearance, it is easy to appreciate that its functions were political as well as military. In this

Himeji Castle-One of the most famous Japanese castles

respect it mirrors the shift in Europe from castles to structures that were intended to be of political as well as military significance.

The Japanese today like views in which a castle can be seen. They like to climb a tenshukaku which soars into the sky and look down on the town around the castle, imagining perhaps, that they have become the lord of the castle. After all, castles were usually constructed in the centre of a piece of territory so the view from the tenshukaku of each castle is bound to be good. So even when the original tenshukaku has long since been destroyed, it often happens that a modern replica is constructed out of reinforced concrete on the original site and used both to house a museum and to offer superb views of the surrounding city. In extreme cases castles have been constructed for tourist purposes in sites where historically there never has been a castle. This can be put down to the fondness of the Japanese for castles: the meaning that castles have today for the Japanese in an age of peace is not as symbols of military might but as urban landmarks.

TANI-Naoki

▎Mediaeval Cities

"The town of Sakai is exceedingly large and many great merchants live there. Like Venice, it is governed by its own administrators."

These are the words of a European missionary who visited Japan some time around the middle of the sixteenth century. It is interesting that he compared it with Venice, one of the most important free cities of medieval Europe.

In the middle ages Venice became known as the most highly developed of the southern European city states and it had won its right to self-government against a background of flourishing trade and lively commercial activity. In the year 1310 the famous Council of Ten was established to administer the city and the city's administration became republican in character. At the same time in Cologne and the other cities of northern Europe, the bishops and feudal landowners were being replaced by the city councils and local citizens.

The special character of these European free cities was shared by Sakai in Japan for a short while. Sakai served as the port for Nara and Kyoto, and it amassed a prodigious amount of wealth through the trade its merchants conducted with China and the so-called 'Southern Barbarians', or in other words, the Europeans! The power conferred by this wealth made it possible for the representatives of the townspeople to take over the running of Sakai and the administration of justice there for themselves. Sakai managed to keep its independent character intact through the wars of the sixteenth century and developed its own system of laws. Daimyo and generals at war with each other were said to have behaved cordially towards each other once they had set foot within the city, though once they were a stone's throw from the borders of the town they would be at each other's throats. The inhabitants of Sakai were determined to lead a peaceful life within the boundaries of their town, and to that end built up the town and its administrative bodies themselves.

Sakai, then, managed to survive the warring of the sixteenth century with its individual concept of a city that was self-governing within and ready to defend itself against outside attacks. Surrounding the town were ramparts and deep moats. There were gates at the points of entry, and these were shut and guarded at night and during times of disturbance. It thus had much in common with the European cities that surrounded themselves with walls of stone or brick as a measure of self-defence and protection.

In Sakai, the street corners and the precincts of temples and shrines fulfilled the same function as the squares or plazas of European cities, serving as spaces where performances and shows of all sorts were constantly being held. On occasion groups of dancers gave what amounted to an exhibition of pride in the town's prosperity and its spirit of solidarity.

A sutra hall in one of the temples of the town was used as the assembly place for the thirty-six representatives of the townspeople, who met and deliberated there regularly. Again this suggests a comparison with the European cities, where a speaker's platform would be erected in the main square under the tower of the town hall and the citizens would conduct their deliberations on matters of importance to the city. The assembly place in Sakai also functioned as a kind of community centre, and in 1566 Christmas was even celebrated there. At that time there were two contingents of rival armies quartered in the town, and many of the samurai belonging to them were Christians. More than seventy of them from both armies attended the Christmas mass and it is said that they treated each other with friendliness and courtesy. It is a token of Sakai's character as a free city that they were able to come together to celebrate Christmas in this way without the usual distinctions between friend and foe.

There are further points of similarity between Japan and Europe in the care which went into the organization of the daily lives of the inhabitants. In both Sakai and Kyoto, town regulations were framed so as to facilitate the smooth running of urban life. It was forbidden, for example, to construct two-storeyed buildings or to hold displays of goods in the streets, and there were rules prescribing how the drainage channels were to be maintained. Such measures as these bespeak a desire to make the urban environment attractive to the eye and once again they call to mind the town regulations in European cities where the cleanliness of the streets was made the responsibility of the households fronting on to them and wells and water-pumps were subject to supervision.

The local independence enjoyed by Sakai spread at the end of the sixteenth century to other cities in various parts of Japan. At times when that independence was threatened, there were even alliances between cities in the interests of mutual defence. In 1568, for example, Oda Nobunaga, with Kyoto already within his grasp, ordered the inhabitants of Sakai to provide funds for his armies, but the townspeople resolved to reject these demands and to prepare to resist any forces he might send. They sent an appeal to a nearby town that also enjoyed some of the character of a free city and proposed that the two should cooperate for the purposes of defence. At this point Oda decided to abandon his attempt against Sakai and he withdrew his armies. The spirit that lay behind Sakai's response to the threat from Oda is similar to the spirit that informed the activities of the Hanseatic League.

Sakai's prosperity as a free city lasted only one hundred years before coming to an end. Now, some four hundred years later, Sakai retains almost nothing of its past. But thirty kilometres to the east of Sakai there is a town called Imai which once also enjoyed some of the features of a free city and was engaged in trade with Sakai. It is a small town, with a population of 4000, but it does preserve the aspect and atmosphere it enjoyed in the sixteenth century and careful thought is now being given to its preservation as a town of historical importance. The preservation of such towns is now a matter that is attracting attention in many countries of the world and it has prompted some international cooperation through the United Nations Organization. Perhaps it will not be long before Imai and the famous West German town of Rotenburg come together to declare an alliance of historical towns.

TANI-Naoki

¹Trade with the Continent

Being surrounded on all sides by water, Japan has long found the sea a hindrance in furthering its communications with its Asian neighbours. The sea has enclosed Japanese in their island country, but at the same time has also served as a moat discouraging those neighbours from seeking to invade Japan.

During the Chinese Sung (960-1279) and Ming (1368-1644) dynasties, Japanese trade with China made great progress and became increasingly international in scope. A considerable number of Japanese ships were engaged in illicit trade and when business was poor they sometimes turned to piracy instead, with the result that Japanese pirates were feared all over China and on the Korean peninsula. On their masts these pirates carried pennants dedicated to Hachiman Daibosatsu, a deity supposed to bring good fortune in war. This is similar to the Spanish practice of sailing the seven seas with the image of the Virgin Mary on their masts. In both cases the objective was to seize what treasure there was to be had and at the same time enjoy divine protection.

But some of these pirates were Chinese, and Chinese pirates came to be more and more numerous as the years went by, eventually, it is said, accounting for some seventy per cent of all the pirates in East Asian waters. Even the chief of the pirates based in Kyushu, the southernmost of Japan's four main islands, was Chinese, and under him were many men who had originally come from southern China. The Ming government had traditionally forbidden Chinese to sail overseas, but it was becoming increasingly hard-

pressed and in 1567 relaxed some of the regulations as to permit trading voyages and voyages
for other purposes to the south. Sailing to Japan
continued to be forbidden, however, for Japan
was considered to be a pirate stronghold. This
state of affairs encouraged Chinese traders to
make their way to the countries of South-East
Asia, and there in time communities of overseas
Chinese became established.

Shut out from China, Japanese ships passed
China by and went on southwards, and there engaged in casual trade with Chinese they encountered in various parts of South-East Asia. It was at
just this time, in the sixteenth century, that Japan
was in the process of being unified and falling
under the rule of a national government. In order
to bring the foreign trade under their control and
at the same time to suppress piracy, Japan's new
rulers issued sailing certificates to bona fide
traders. Over thirty years or so from the end of
the sixteenth century to the beginning of the
seventeenth century Japanese trading ships
issued with these certificates flocked down to the
ports of South-East Asia. The certificates were
stamped with a vermilion seal, and so the ships
that carried them, that is the ships that were
licensed to trade, were known as 'shuinsen', or
'vermilion-seal ships'.

The age of the licensed ships coincided with the
end of the European age of the great voyages.
From the west the Portuguese had now reached
South-East Asia and were establishing settlements wherever they went and thus expanding
the boundaries and volume of their trade. They
were followed by the Spanish, the Dutch, the English and the French. They all moved gradually
northwards and eventually reached China and

Japan. By this time Japan had abandoned its passive stance and was adopting a more active one. Licensed ships were being sent further and further to the south, and South-East Asia became the area where Japanese conducted casual trade not so much now with Chinese as with various Europeans.

The result of the trading activities of the licensed ships was the emergence of a class of traders in Japan and the formation of a bourgeoisie. The great merchants of Kyoto, Sakai, Nagasaki and other such cities joined with the government in providing the necessary finance. Among these 'licensed ship' traders were some foreigners, such as Will Adams of England and Jan Josten of the Netherlands. They had both boarded the 'Liefde', a Dutch vessel, in Europe and after crossing the Atlantic and the Pacific had drifted ashore in Japan. This was in 1600. Adams later became an adviser on international relations to Tokugawa Ieyasu, the first shogun of the Edo period; he was granted land in Miura and even took a Japanese name, Miura Anjin, the word 'anjin' meaning a ships pilot. Adams made a great contribution to the growth of trade between England and Japan and he eventually died in Japan. He was a symbol of the first stage of Anglo-Japanese friendship.

To return to the licensed ships, it appears from available evidence that they numbered at least three hundred and fifty. The countries they sailed to included the modern Philippines, Viet-Nam, Cambodia, Thailand, and most of South-East Asia: foremost amongst these was Thailand. Each ship carried a crew of three hundred or thereabouts, so more than one hundred thousand Japanese must have travelled overseas during this period. At the ports they sailed to Japanese towns developed which were allowed to be self-governing: the townspeople elected their own representatives. The trade conducted between Japan and these ports was very lively indeed. The imports brought to Japan by the licensed ships included raw cotton, silk goods, deerskins, molasses and various artefacts from distant Europe too. Japanese exports included silver, copper, sulphur and other minerals, as well as fans, screens and lacquerware. Such export items as chests and cabinets had overall European designs, but they were decorated with Japanese tortoise-shell work or metal inlay. Lacquerware was the major export item during this period, and just as porcelain was known as 'china', so too lacquer was known as 'japan', and both were equally highly valued. In 1618 the director of the English trading mission in Japan recorded in his diary that he had placed an order for a large quantity of lacquerware. Even now in the audience room in Windsor Castle there is Japanese export lacquerware alongside European furniture.

The energy of the Japanese nation began to bloom in an international way in the seventeenth century. If this had continued to develop, the Japanese economy would without doubt have left an important historical mark on the world economy at that time. But the age of the licensed ships lasted not even a full thirty years before coming to an end, for the bakufu government opted for a policy of national seclusion. For the following two centuries the energy of the Japanese vanished without trace from the international stage.

TANI-Naoki

Gold and Silver

Columbus was unable to realize his dream of sailing westwards across the Atlantic as far as Cipangu, Marco Polo's name for Japan, and amassing there huge quantities of gold and silver. But Spain, which had provided the financial backing for his voyage, had similar dreams of gold and silver and his discovery of the New World made these dreams grow much greater. After the Spaniards had landed in Mexico and Peru, they discovered some of the world's richest underground deposits of gold and silver. The Potosi silver mine, for example, which was discovered in 1545, was one of the largest silver mines there have ever been. The Spaniards rounded up large numbers of the native Indians to extract the gold and silver. Their labours made it possible for enormous quantities of gold and silver to be sent from the New World back to Spain. So large were the quantities of silver sent back that in the latter half of the sixteenth century currency values in Europe lost their equilibrium and there were steep rises in the cost of living. No small amount of silver could have caused such harm.

At the very same time Japan had also become a major producer of silver on a par with Mexico and Peru. The figures can be left until later - let us first look at the place of gold and silver in Japan in the sixteenth century. At that time, Japan was being plagued with civil wars and disturbances, and many of the daimyo were fighting with each other in their determination to get to the capital, Kyoto, and bring the whole country under their sway. Thanks to the development of an economy based on commerce, currency in gold and silver was now circulating to a certain extent and it was beginning to attract attention as a means of coping with military expenses, for it was easier to transport and handle than rice. Having come to this realisation, the daimyo of the sixteenth century gave positive encouragement to the development and exploitation of mines within their territories. Examples of such daimyo mines are the Takeda gold mine in Kurokawa, the Uesugi Tsuruko gold mine on the island of Sado, the Ouchi silver mine at Omori, and the Yamana silver mine at Ikuno. Work was begun on the silver mine at Omori in 1533 and here a new method of refining silver was developed. This was the cupellation method for gold and silver ore containing lead. The ore is placed in an ashen hearth (cupel) in a furnace; the lead oxidizes and sinks to the ash at the bottom, enabling the gold or silver to be removed. This method of refining gold and silver very quickly spread to all parts of Japan and by the end of the sixteenth century it had reached such a high level that the Catholic missionary Juan Rodrigues recorded with amazement the excellence of the refining techniques in Japanese silver mines.

The civil wars were eventually brought to an end by Oda Nobunaga, whose soldiers had mastered the use of firearms which had recently been introduced to Japan. He took control of the Ikuno mine and stored large quantities of gold and silver at his castle in Azuchi. After his death Toyotomi Hideyoshi took over where he had left off, brought the gold mines of Sado and the Omori silver mine under his control as well, and made much of the gold and silver produced throughout the country his own. It must indeed have seemed as if "gold and silver mines have sprung up all over Japan since Hideyoshi came to power", as a contemporary wrote. Hideyoshi did not neglect to make political use of the gold and silver he had amassed. In 1589 he filled one of his castles with gold and silver and summoned the court nobles and the daimyo of the land one by one to receive presents. It is recorded that on this occasion he gave away six thousand pieces of gold and twenty-five thousand pieces of silver. However, since records for the year 1598 reveal that his income from the gold and silver mines for that year amounted to 3397 pieces of gold and 79,415 pieces of silver, it is clear that his gifts amounted to a small proportion of the coinage at his disposal.

The Ginza in Tokyo is well-known throughout the world as one of Japan's most prosperous and exciting shopping areas, but it is not so widely known that the name means 'silver mint'. It was given this name by Tokugawa Ieyasu, who took over the reins of power after the death of Hideyoshi. After establishing his castle in Edo (Tokyo), he set up an office and factory there for the minting of the bakufu's silver coinage, and this was known as the 'ginza'. At that time there were other 'ginzas' in Osaka and Nagasaki as well, and the Nagasaki mint in particular was responsible for supervising the expenditure of silver coinage used for settling foreign trade accounts. The 'shuinsen' or ships licensed for trading by the bakufu, used to set out for China and other countries with a cargo of some 2000 kilograms of silver per ship. Since on average ten to fifteen vessels would leave each year, and more than double that number during the period when this trade was at its peak, it is apparent that in some years as many as sixty thousand kilograms of silver were being loaded onto the ships. The Portuguese ships carried similar amounts of silver away with them each year, and when the silver taken by Dutch and Chinese ships is taken into account as well, it can be estimated that the amount of silver leaving the country came to 150,000 kilograms in some years. At about this time 370,000 kilograms of silver reached Spain in one year for which records have survived, and from this figure it is easy to grasp just how important Japanese silver was in world trade at that time.

Although they were, like Japan, producers of silver, Mexico, Peru and the other countries of South America were colonies of the great European powers and so they derived suffering rather than wealth from their mines. If Columbus had managed to reach Japan as he had planned, either Spain or one of the other European powers might have mined a lot of gold or silver in Japan; and Japan might possibly have become a colony and have been made subject to foreign rule, and her relations with Europe might have begun on an inauspicious note. There were two factors which were probably crucial in preventing this: one was Japan's geographical position, for whether approached from the west or the east, Japan was simply too far away from the European colonial powers; and the other was the historical chance that Japan's discovery was delayed for half a century, which gave such outstanding figures as Oda Nobunaga and Hideyoshi the time to bring about the unification of the country. Be that as it may, some three hundred years after Marco Polo travelled the Silk Road to China and told Europeans of Cipangu, the island of gold, the development of the silver trade established the first links between Japan and Europe.

TANI-Naoki

⅃Guns and Muskets

On the twenty-fifth day of the eighth month of 1543, a large ship drifted ashore on the island of Tanegashima, off the south coast of Kyushu. The ship was full of Portuguese who had with them things the islanders had never seen before, long tubes which had an opening at one end. Sometimes fire would come out of the open end and the islanders would hear a loud report like a thunderclap, and straightaway a bird that had been flying up in the air would fall to earth dead. One of the islanders lost no time in informing Tokitaka, the lord of the island, of what he had seen. Tokitaka entertained the Portuguese and treated them with great kindness and he was finally able, though at great cost, to purchase one of these amazing tubes. This was the very first stage in the introduction of firearms to Japan, and the events are recorded as they have been described above in a Japanese chronicle relating to firearms, *Teppo-ki*. European records indicate that the Portuguese reached Japan in 1542, and so there is a discrepancy of one year between the two accounts. But leaving aside the tangled question of the date, this was an epoch-making confrontation for the Japanese of the sixteenth century. Until then Japan's knowledge of the world had been limited to the countries of East Asia, but now it suddenly came into direct contact with the European world and set eyes on firearms for the first time.

According to the *Teppo-ki*, Tokitaka ordered his swordsmith to make a gun on the model of the one he had bought from the Portuguese. After expending great efforts, the swordsmith was finally able to fashion a barrel, but he could not discover how to block up one end of the barrel satisfactorily. He obtained instructions from a Portuguese blacksmith who chanced to reach the island on a sailing ship the following year, and had the secret explained to him. It was necessary, he learnt, to block the breech by screwing in a stopper, for nothing else would be able to withstand the explosive force of the gunpowder. In Europe screwing devices had been used for pressing grapes since the days of the Greek and Roman empires, but in Japan levers had been used for similar types of work and so the screw was unknown to Japanese. Consequently, knowledge of the screw was another product of these early years of contact with Europeans.

But what is of more importance here than learning about the screw is the fact than on a small island, far from the capital, Japanese had acquired firearms, a product of the latest European technology, and had set about manufacturing them for themselves. To explain this it is not enough to say simply that the Japanese were imitating what they found, for without a relatively high level of technology to start with it would have been impossible to manufacture firearms in Japan at all. Half a century before the first guns reached Tanegashima, Japanese iron manufature had undergone something of a technological revolution and by the middle of the sixteenth century Japan was producing iron that was by no means inferior to the products of the iron-making technology in Europe. The fine forging techniques that were used for the production of Japanese swords could readily, it was found, be adapted to suit the manufacture of gun barrels. Japanese swords were already being exported in large numbers to China and they had acquired a good reputation there; the sword-making technology of Japan had reached such a level by then that the European missionaries who came to Japan at this time were awed and amazed by the sharp cutting edge of the Japanese sword.

To turn to *Teppo-ki* again, it is recorded that in just over a year it proved possible to manufacture several dozen Japanese matchlocks. This was no mean a small achievement in view of the fact that nobody had been able to do this either in India or in China. Once production of firearms had started in Japan, the technology spread throughout the country with surprising speed. Sakai, in modern Osaka Prefecture, Negoro in Wakayama Prefecture, and Kunitomo in Shiga Prefecture had all been areas where swordsmiths had long been active already, but now they became the three main areas for the manufacture of Japanese firearms as the swordsmiths developed and applied the skills they had already acquired. The increasing production of firearms meant that before long they were to be found all over the country.

Meanwhile, the introduction of firearms was completely revolutionizing Japanese conceptions of military strategy. The sixteenth century was a time of civil wars and ferment, and the warriors in all the provinces were fighting tooth and nail to get hold of the new weapons. But in fact some thirty years had to elapse before strategies were to develop, based on the possession of firearms, and it was Oda Nobunaga who had a crucial role to play in their development. Nobunaga's forces came up against those of Takeda Katsuyori in the battle of Nagashino in 1575. The climax of Akira Kurosawa's film *Kagemusha*, which won the Grand Prix at Cannes in 1981, is based on this battle. Takeda's forces consisted mainly of brigades of mounted knights and their ferocious assaults were feared throughout the land. Nobunaga, however, erected wooden palisades to keep Takeda's mounted warriors at bay, and behind them he put three thousand soldiers armed with matchlocks. The guns in use at that time had to be loaded with ball and powder from the muzzle and could only be fired after the musketeer had blown on the tinder to enable it to ignite the gunpowder fuse, had taken up his weapon and had then applied the tinder to the breech. Since this had to be repeated for each shot, continuous firing was impossible, and so the soldiers were divided up into three groups firing in rotation. The approach of Takeda's horsemen was the signal to open fire, but Nobunaga's matchlock-men waited until they were close to the palisades before opening fire with a thousand guns at a time. Although the weapons were only effective up to one hundred metres and had an accuracy of just sixty to seventy per cent, they were still able to inflict a terrible amount of damage, and Takeda's forces were finally scattered in all directions. Whereas Takeda's forces had been composed of warriors, mainly mounted on horseback, Nobunaga's matchlock-men were ordinary soldiers of the lowest rank. The loss of many of his finest horsemen naturally dealt Takeda's army a grievous blow.

This battle in the end revolutionized Japanese warfare and ushered in an age during which strategy was based on squads of low-ranking matchlock-men. Nobunaga's deployment of the new weapon and his development of a new strategy to go with it eventually enabled him to bring the wars to an end and achieve the unification of the country.

TANI-Naoki

Marco Polo

"Cipangu is an island far out to sea about fifteen hundred miles from Manzi. It is a very big island....[The people there] are idolaters, and they subordinate themselves to no other state. It is said that they have gold in great abundance, but the reason for this is they mine gold on the island and their king forbids the gold to be exported. Also, since it is far from the mainland, hardly any traders visit it, and so the amount of gold they have in their possession is very great indeed."

This is part of the section in *The Travels of Marco Polo* that deals with Japan. The word 'Cipangu' used by Marco Polo comes from the name by which Japan was known in China at that time, and it means 'the country of the rising sun'. It is also the origin of the words for Japan in English, German, and other European languages.

Marco Polo left Venice for the Far East in 1271. He made his way to Central Asia by way of Jerusalem and Baghdad and then he followed the old silk road on to China. In 1275 he had an audience with Khubilai Khan. His stay in China lasted for seventeen years, after which he returned to Europe by sea, reaching Venice again in 1295.

It was the age of the crusades in Europe and interest in the East was growing, and in Asia the nomadic Mongol peoples had founded the Chinese Yüan Dynasty and built a huge empire that covered most of Eurasia. Since the days of the Greek and Roman empires stories had been handed down of islands of gold and silver in the eastern oceans. So it was in the natural course of events that Marco Polo's account of his years in the East should have aroused great interest and curiosity among his contemporaries.

But for two hundred and fifty years after Marco Polo's return to Europe, Cipangu, the island of gold, remained nothing more than an island that was fascinating from afar, but no European set foot there. Europe was, however, entering the age of the great voyages of exploration and discovery, and in 1486 the southern tip of Africa was discovered and named the Cape of Good Hope. In 1498 a squadron of ships led by Vasco da Gama, whose voyages had the support of the Portuguese throne, rounded the Cape and reached India, thus opening up the sea route to the East. It now became possible for Europeans to buy the spices of the orient directly from Indian merchants rather than having to go through Arab traders as they had done until then, and the profits from this new trade were enormous. Within another twenty years the Portuguese had sailed further east to the Malay Peninsula and the southern coast of China. Ningpo, a port in southern China, had long been one of the outlets from which Chinese exports were sent to Japan. So Japan was now within arm's reach.

Spain, meanwhile, was searching for a different route to the orient and the profits it offered, than the one that was being pioneered by the Portuguese. The geographer Toscanelli had put forward the novel theory that the world was round and, although nobody had yet been able to offer any proof, the Italian Christopher Columbus believed that he was right and argued that the shortest way to the Indies from Europe would therefore lie to the west. Queen Isabella of Spain gave her support to Columbus' expedition and in 1492 his three ships reached dry land on the other side of the Atlantic Ocean. This was the discovery of the New World. At the time, however, Columbus seems not to have realized that he had landed in the New World and was convinced that he had reached Marco Polo's Cipangu. He had carried with him on the voyage a copy of a Latin translation of *The Travels of Marco Polo*; this is now preserved in the Columbus Library in Spain and it is said to contain notes written in his own hand in forty-five places. Given that Toscanelli's map of the world would have led anyone to suppose that sailing west from Europe would bring one straight to the eastern part of the Asiatic mainland, Columbus' misunderstanding was inevitable. Whenever he landed, it is said, he questioned the natives about the place names he found recorded in *The Travels of Marco Polo*. So the quest for Cipangu, the island of gold, which Marco Polo had inspired, led to an unexpected result in the form of the discovery of a new continent. Later, in 1519, Ferdinand Magellan, who had taken over the convictions that Columbus had held and also had the support of the Spanish throne behind him like Columbus, opened up a westward route to the East via the straits that bear his name and reached the Philippines after more than a year at sea.

Thus at about the same time both the Spanish and the Portuguese were approaching the seas around Japan, the one from the east the other from the west. The first European to have set foot on Japanese soil is said to have been Portuguese in 1542. What, we may wonder, did he make of the alleged island of gold that had been wondered about for so long? At the end of the thirteenth century, when Marco Polo was in China, Japan was as yet producing neither very much gold nor silver. But from the middle of the six-

teenth century onwards, the production of gold
and silver from mines all over Japan began to increase dramatically. Japan was in fact on the
verge of a kind of gold rush, the like of which was
not to be seen again. Portuguese ships were soon
followed by Spanish, English and Dutch ships,
precisely because the reality of Japan in the sixteenth century was such as not to disappoint their
expectations of an island of gold.

TANI-Naoki

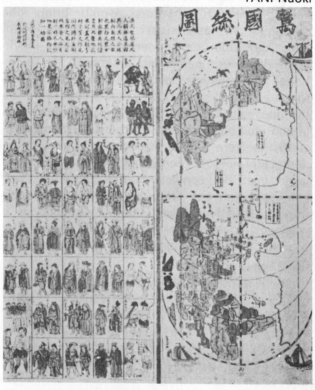

World atlas

Edo, City of a Million

The capital of Japan today is Tokyo. The name 'Tokyo' means 'eastern capital' and the city was given this name in 1868 when the emperor moved there from Kyoto after the Meiji Restoration had been successfully carried out. The new Meiji government used this change of name to indicate that the city was now to be the seat of political power.

Prior to this the city had been called Edo, and with a population of approximately one million it had for some time been the largest city in Japan. The foundation of a settlement on the present site of Tokyo dates back to the sixteenth century when Tokugawa Ieyasu, who was at the time a daimyo but was later to become the first shogun of the Tokugawa bakufu, had a castle constructed there. And in 1603, when Ieyasu was appointed shogun, he decided that his government would be based in Edo. Consequently, the government which was under the control of generations of Tokugawa shoguns is known as the Edo bakufu and the period during which it existed is known as the Edo period.

It is not known why Ieyasu chose Kanto in the east and not Kansai which had traditionally been the center of Japan as the center of his administration. But his decision meant that Japan now had two centers of Kanto and Kansai. Gradually, Kanto overwhelmed Kansai, and the former's superiority became definite as the result of the Meiji Restoration. The urban growth of Edo moved the center of Japan to the east, thus setting a direction for the structure of modern Japan.

During this period, there was an imperial court

in Kyoto consisting of the members of the aristocracy with the emperor at their head and a bakufu in Edo which consisted of samurai and which was presided over by the incumbent shogun. Throughout the Edo period, neither the emperor nor the imperial court had any real influence on the politics of government. The de facto rulers of Japan during the Edo period were the shogun and the administrative structure which was centred around him. In principle, however, the emperor's rank was higher than that of the shogun.

Until the changes brought about by the Meiji Restoration, it was almost as if Japan had had two capitals at the same time for a couple of hundred years, Edo and Kyoto. And in fact there was a common expression referring to the 'three capitals', namely Edo, Kyoto and the commercial city of Osaka.

All the daimyo in Japan were required by the Edo bakufu to attend the shogun's court in Edo every other year. This was the 'sankin kōtai' system, or the system of alternate residence, and it was regarded as a symbol of the loyalty of the daimyo to the shogun. Each daimyo spent one year in his domain in the provinces and the following year he repaired to Edo in the company of a large number of his followers; the next year he once again returned to his home in the provinces. This system differs from both that of France where aristocrats permanently lived in the capital Paris and that of Germany where each feudal lord, in contrast, permanently resided in his own territory. In other words, the system in Japan was a mixture of the above two.

By leaving his domain for Edo, a daimyo did not of course turn his back on the administration of

his territory and a number of his officials remained behind. Since the daimyo were compelled
to spend every other year in Edo, they all constructed their own residences in Edo and had
their families and large numbers of followers live
there on a permanent basis. There is no doubt
that for the daimyo it was an enormous financial
burden to have to maintain two households in
their domains and in Edo, but it is also true that
the frequent movement of large numbers of
samurai about Japan in this way enabled the culture of all of Japan's provinces to reach Edo and
the culture of Edo to reach the provinces. In this
way Edo functioned as a melting-pot in which
provincial culture was absorbed, stirred around
and then redistributed to the provinces.

The territories of the daimyo were all independent miniature states, each one with its different
characteristics, but at the same time they all had
close ties with Edo at the centre of Japan through
the sankin-kotai network. It is not going too far to
say that this was one of the bases for the formation of the modern Japanese nation-state.

Edo was a place in which vast numbers of
samurai were gathered throughout the year and
so it is not surprising that it should be referred to
as a man's town, one in which men predomin-
ated. Of course the closed society of Edo consisted of more than just the samurai. They gradually came to be on familiar terms with the chonin or townsmen living in Edo. These townsmen
would not have been able to make their livings
without the samurai who formed the consumer
population of Edo, and they also gained many
employment opportunities from the existence of
the samurai households, including domestic service. In addition, there were many opportunities

for samurai and townsmen to mix in public - excursions in each season of the year, play-going, visits to the Yoshiwara pleasure quarter, and so on.

Some who were samurai devoted themselves to the theatres, while others who were townsmen bought for themselves the rank and privileges of a samurai. The father of the Navy Minister during the Meiji Restoration had been a townsman who bought for himself the rank of a samurai. Society was so organized at the time that samurai and townsmen were supposed to be different classes and as a consequence of this the cultures of these two classes were supposed to be different, but in cases like these it was impossible to say which was which. So at the same time as being a centre where cultures from the provinces were mixed together, Edo was also a place where the differences between the samurai and townsmen classes were eroded and a new urban culture came into being. Kyoto was also a town which had a tradition of urban culture, but whereas this was a culture formed by aristocrats and townsmen, the urban culture of Edo was by contrast one which expressed much more clearly the characteristics of urban cultures.

MORIYA-Takeshi

Shoguns

The word 'shogun' is a title indicating the position of chief officer of the bakufu, that is to say, of chief officer of a government in the hands of the warriors.

Originally shogun was nothing more than the title of a temporary official post attached to the imperial court in the distant past, in the Heian period, nearly a thousand years ago. The post was that of commander-in-chief of the armies which were seeking to subjugate the unruly peoples who lived on the borderlands of the areas administered by the central government under the emperor and who would not submit to his authority . The man nominated to the post of shogun was responsible for leading an expeditionary force of warriors to the northeastern parts of the country, and it is probably only on such occasions that the shogun enjoyed the position of being head and shoulders above the other warriors. But the warriors at that time were in fact merely the servants of the court aristocracy, and the post of shogun was simply one that could be given to such a warrior, and that too merely temporarily.

It was in the twelfth and thirteenth centuries that the position of shogun came to indicate the leader of a government conducted by the warriors and not by the court. After having won victory in the civil strife of the twelfth century, Minamoto Yoritomo sought appointment from the emperor as shogun, and when this request was granted he established a bakufu, or military government, in Kamakura, near present-day Tokyo. For the warriors as a whole, this meant that they had managed to rise above their position in service to the court aristocracy and had now established themselves as a political power in their own right. This new alignment was an accurate reflection of the military power which groups of warriors all over the country had exercised during the preceding years of civil war.

From this time onwards it became the custom for a man whose military might had brought the whole country under his control to be named shogun, to establish a bakufu government, and then for his office to be subject to hereditary succession. Thus the Muromachi bakufu was established by a new shogun, Ashikaga Takauji, who had fought his way through the wars of the fourteenth century, and then later, Tokugawa Ieyasu, who brought the strife of the sixteenth century to an end, established his own bakufu, the Edo bakufu. The shogun can in each case reasonably be said to have been the leader of the military group which had fought with him in the wars from which he had emerged victorious. These powerful warriors accepted the strongest daimyo amongst them as their shogun and took official positions in the bakufu government he then established.

Several of the Ashikagas, however, who were the hereditary shoguns of the Muromachi bakufu, maintained close connections with the emperor and the court aristocracy. And there were also cases like that of Toyotomi Hideyoshi, who, although he had brought the whole country under his sway, did not aspire to the position of shogun on account of his wish for aristocratic advancement. Such examples as these show that there was still a strong attachment to the aristocracy among the warriors.

Originally, the bakufu, a government of warriors with a shogun at its head, was a body which exerted authority over the warrior class and at the same time represented its interests. In time however, it came to take the place of the government of emperor and aristocrats, which had gradually been losing its administrative ability, and to exercise de facto control over the whole country. In particular, under the Edo bakufu the authority of the Tokugawa shoguns was such as to render the emperor powerless. At the time of its establisment the Edo bakufu was a military form of government with the shogun at its centre and the basis of the shogun's authority was the unsurpassed military prowess and wealth of the Tokugawas. Soon, however, the shogun's authority was enhanced by the bakufu's organised administrative machinery, the administrative abilities of the warrior-bureaucrats who constituted its members, and the loyalty of the daimyo in all parts of the country.

Since the position of shogun had originated in an official court title, it was the rule that the title was conferred by the emperor: the understanding was that the shogun was ruling the land with the authority bestowed upon him by the emperor. In the early days of the Edo bakufu this rule was at least nominally adhered to and the shoguns were appointed by the emperor. However, it became the custom for the Tokugawas to succeed to the shogunate one after the other, and the practise of having the emperor appoint the shogun came to an end. The Tokugawas simply chose a new shogun from amongst themselves without even consulting the emperor: neither the emperor nor anybody else found any fault with this arrangement. In the court the position of shogun was struck off the list of appointments to be made, and from this point onwards it is proper to speak of the Edo bakufu and the Tokugawa shoguns as being independent of the court.

For all his power, however, the shogun never once tried to abolish the system of emperor and court government. The founder of the Muromachi bakufu, Ashikaga Takauji, was drawn into confrontation with the emperor of the day and was even in a state of civil war with him, but he simply replaced him with another emperor. The result of this was that during the fourteenth century there were for a while two imperial courts in existence at the same time, but ultimately the emperor and his court survived as institutions.

Thus, throughout the Kamakura, Muromachi and Edo periods, there were two governments coexisting in one and the same country - the court, composed of aristocrats who could trace their lines of descent back to the Heian period and earlier, which represented prestige and authority, and the bakufu, composed of warriors in bureaucratic roles, which exercised the real secular political power. It may well be that the relationship between the court and bakufu in Japan is a parallel to the relationship between the Roman Catholic Church and the secular political authorities in Europe.

The Meiji Restoration took the form of a return to the monarchical system of pre-Kamakura times and the abdication of the shogun brought to an end the system of dual government.

MORIYA-Takeshi

Roads and Communications

The development of communications and the frequent movement of people about the country have, since well before the Edo period, been characteristic of Japanese society. In the mediaeval period, local barons in the provinces set up barriers on the roads and rivers in their territories and made people travelling through the areas under their jurisdiction pay a tax for the right of passage. Historians assert that this impeded the development of communications, and there can be no doubt that these barriers did in fact constitute a hindrance to the development of communications. On the other hand, however, the very existence of these barriers in the distant past indicates at the very least that there was a sufficient volume of traffic to make it worthwhile to think of deriving an income from such taxes. The existence of large numbers of these barriers throughout Japan in the middle ages has therefore to be seen as a phenomenon that is in accord with a large amount of traffic along the roads of the country.

The establishment of the Edo bakufu at the beginning of the seventeenth century brought with it further developments in the movement of people and goods throughout the country. The bakufu saw to the construction and maintenance of major highways connecting the main centres of population and to the rapid development of post towns along the highways. Particular importance was attached to the five highways branching out from Edo, which was the political capital of Japan at the time.

The most important of these highways was undoubtedly the Tokaido, which more or less followed the coastline as it stretched from Edo to the old capital of Kyoto. Trees were planted by the side of the road, a mound serving as a milestone was constructed at every other village, and a total of fifty-three post towns was constructed along the way. The Sanyōdo constituted a continuation of the Tokaido which took travellers down to the island of Kyushu: it was not one of the so-called 'big five' highways, but together with the Tokaido it formed the major route of travel in the Edo period, extending from Edo right the way down to Kyushu in the south.

The route followed by the old Tokaido is more or less the same as that followed today by Highway Number One, the Meishin and Tomei Expressways, and the Tokaido Shinkansen, the first of the 'Bullet Train' lines. And Highway Number Two and the Sanyo Shinkansen follow the route taken by the old Sanyodo.Furthermore, most of the major cities of Japan today are to be found along the routes followed by those two highways. Not only were they regarded as central to the communications of Japan in the Edo period, but they have continued to the present day to play an important cultural role.

Moving now from the development of communications on the land, let us turn to the development of communications by sea during the Edo period. Of course, the government during the Edo period pursued a policy of isolationism and so there was no development in the form of long-distance voyages, but an intricate network of sea-routes emerged during this period to connect all the major towns which could be approached from the sea. These sea routes encouraged the development of these towns, and so during the Edo period virtually all the major cities in some form or another managed to flourish as harbour towns as well.

In the case of those major cities which were located inland, most of them enjoyed some connection with the sea by means of a major river. Without such contact with the sea and the communications it offered, it was almost impossible for a city to develop and prosper. Kyoto, for example, was connected with Osaka and the routes passing through the Inland Sea by the boats which used the Yodo River.

These sea-borne routes were intended not so much for the movement of people as for the transportation of large amounts of goods. So areas without access to sea transportation tended to be left out of the spread and circulation of material goods. In Japan it has for centuries been the practice to use ships for the transportation of large quantities of goods. On land the roads were used for the movements of people, whether on foot or on horse-back, and not much attention was given to the possibility of transporting goods by road. This meant that horse-drawn carts and baggage wagons were slow to emerge, but on the other hand it also led to greater developments in coastal shipping and sea transportation.

During the Edo period all the 'han', or feudal domains, needed to convert the rice and other products that they collected as taxes in kind into cash. In order to do this it was necessary to transport the large amounts of rice from the places where they were produced all the way to the central markets where they could be sold. The very survival of those domains located a long way away from the markets depended on long-distance transportation. During the latter half of the seventeenth century and the first half of the eighteenth century private merchants saw to the development of routes of sea transportation connecting the provinces with the central markets of Edo and Osaka - the major ones were the eastern route connecting Edo with northern Japan and the circular western route connecting Osaka with north-western Japan. It was the wholesale merchants of the major cities who were behind this: they formed guilds consisting of their fellow traders, monopolized the new sea routes with the permission of the bakufu and won for themselves enormous profits. Some of them pioneered the development of several new routes and have left their names in the history of Japanese seafaring.

Communications between those cities facing the Japan Sea and Edo or Osaka thus depended to a considerable extent on sea transportation. Ships passing out of Osaka sailed along the Inland Sea until they came out into the Japan Sea and then stopped at the major towns on the coast all the way up to Hokkaido, offloading material goods from Osaka. On their return they gathered the rice and local produce from each area and carried them back to Osaka.

Trade based on sea transportation in this way made it possible for the towns on the Japan Sea to flourish and prosper. This is evident from the fact that during the Edo period the towns with the large populations were to be found not so often along the Tokaido and the Sanyodo as scattered along the Japan Sea coastline.

The exchange of goods also involved cultural exchange as well, and so the culture of Osaka, in particular, thus reached the towns on the Japan Sea. Today traces of the old culture of Osaka can still be found in some of these coastal towns.

MORIYA-Takeshi

⚓The Han and the Daimyo

Under the Edo bakufu, the shogun gave territorial domains to the powerful samurai or daimyo who supported the bakufu and the shogun, and entrusted to them the administration of their domains. The scale of an individual domain was indicated by its 'kokudaka', or total agricultural yield expressed in terms of bushels of rice. The size of the 'kokudaka' of a given domain was related to the amount of tax revenue gained by the daimyo, and this meant that the higher the 'kokudaka' the richer the daimyo was.

At the same time, however, daimyo had to shoulder a number of responsibilities put upon them by the bakufu, such as dispatching troops when it was necessary to put down an internal disturbance or assistance with public works projects undertaken by the bakufu; these duties were allotted in accordance with the 'kokudaka' of the various daimyo. Thus daimyo administering territories with a high 'kokudaka' had a higher share of such duties to bear.

The daimyo during the Edo period were ranked in a complicated order of priority dependent upon the 'kokudaka' of their territories and upon how close they were to the family of the shogun. Daimyo close to the shogun's family had low 'kokudaka' but their territories were sited in important areas such as the eastern seaboard between Edo and Osaka the area around Nara and Kyoto. Daimyo who were distant from the shogun's family had territories which had comparatively high 'kokudaka' but were situated in more remote areas. It is worth pointing out here that the Meiji Restoration, which brought the Edo

Castle town (Hagi-City. Yamaguchi prefecture)

bakufu to an end, was promoted and brought into effect by vassals of these daimyo from the more remote domains.

Just as the bakufu constructed the castle and city of Edo and made it the focal point of its rule, so the greater part of the daimyo also built castles in their domains and castle towns to accompany them. The vassals of the daimyo lived in the castle towns and constituted a system of local government which had the daimyo at its head. The custom of referring to the territories of the daimyo and their local governments as 'han' in contrast with a central government going by the name of the bakufu, dates from the eighteenth century. And the state during the Edo period is thus referred to as the 'bakuhan' system, one composed of the bakufu and the han in a delicate balance of powers.

The han were of course under the control of the bakufu: they were not allowed to mobilize their forces, and contact between the han was subject to various restrictions. However, the han also enjoyed a certain measure of political independence from the bakufu. The laws and ordinances of the bakufu only had actual effect in the territories under the direct control of the bakufu itself,

and the officials of the bakufu could only intervene in the politics of the han in times of
emergency. Although in general all the han applied the bakufu's laws in their own domains,
nevertheless each had its own independent body
of law as well and appointed its own officials for
the business of local administration. They were
thus miniature states modelled on the pattern of
the bakufu.

It is reasonable to say that local self-
government in modern Japan is based on the
tradition of the local han administrations. This is
evident from the fact that the offices of local self-
government in most of the present-day prefectures of Japan are sited in cities that were during
the Edo period the castle towns of the local han.

Han finances were based on taxes paid by the
peasants in the domain in the form of rice and on
compulsory donations paid in cash by the merchants in the castle town. This was similar to the
finances of the bakufu, which were based on the
taxes derived from the territories under the bakufu's own control and on money raised from merchants. The bakufu, of course, gave the han no
financial help, and the han in their turn did not
have to make any regular payments to the bakufu. Economically too, the han were akin to small
independent states.

The rule was that the peasants' taxes had to be
paid in rice and this rice was distributed among
the vassals of the han as a form of annual salary.
Of course, there was no other important source of
income to speak of and if all of this rice was used
as food neither the han nor its vassals could continue to exist. So a part of the rice was kept aside
for food and the rest was converted into cash at
the rice markets in Osaka and elsewhere. Every-

day goods had to be bought with the cash thus obtained. Thus the changes in the current price of rice at the central markets was a matter of very great concern to the people in each han who were in charge of the han finances.

Since the 'kokudaka' was simply the theoretical productive capacity of the han territory measured in rice, the actual harvests did not necessarily equal the amount of the fixed 'kokudaka'. In practice, the income derived from taxes would often be far lower than the 'kokudaka' would have led one to expect. There were in fact few han which could manage their financial affairs solely by means of the taxes on the peasants, and most of them gradually sunk into worse and worse economic difficulties.

Some han, however, promoted the development of various other kinds of agricultural production to ease their financial situation. They developed products that were suited to the climate and geographical features of the region in which they were situated - in one han it would be wax, in an other lacquer, paper or salt - and the han supervised the production and marketing of these products. The result of this was that the han as a whole came to have the character of a modern industrial enterprise.

Modern Japanese enterprises today still retain the tradition of securing the cooperation and agreement of all individual members in the activities of the firm, a tradition developed by the han. And, to give an extreme example, the official titles of positions in modern business enterprises, such as 'torishimariyaku' (managing director) and 'juyaku' (director), derive from the titles used for official positions in the han.

MORIYA-Takeshi

The Ideology of the Samurai

The political ideology which the bakufu took as its basis during the Edo period was Confucianism, a philosophy that had originally developed in Ancient China. Owing to its adoption and enforcement by the bakufu government, the influence of Confucianism is thought to have spread beyond the society of the samurai, who constituted the ruling class, and to have reached every corner of Japanese society. Further it has been argued by some people that the moral beliefs and values of the Japanese people today contain a number of elements that can be traced back to the Confucian values that became established in Japan in the course of the Edo period, and most Japanese believe these arguments to be well-founded.

But these widely-held views need to be seriously questioned on at least two counts. The first relates to just how committed the bakufu really was to Confucianism, and the second to the actual nature of the ideas that the Japanese today understand to be Confucian. These questions have to be posed because when Japan is compared to other countries of East Asia that also took Confucianism as a kind of political basis at about the same time, it has to be admitted that Japanese Confucianism was far from being an authentic version of the original philosophy.

It is true enough that the bakufu regarded Confucianism, and especially that branch of it known in Japanese as Shushigaku (after the Chinese philosopher Chu Hsi), as the only orthodox form of learning. And it is also a fact that the successive heads of the Hayashi family were in the service of the bakufu as Confucian scholars. However, the bakufu only made the Hayashi family's private academy into a centre of learning under the control of the bakufu in the second half of the Edo period, at the end of the eighteenth century. Following the example of the bakufu, each han also set about establishing its own school and promoting Confucian education within the area under its authority. There are thought to have been some 280 such han schools throughout the country in the Edo period, but more than half of them were not founded until some time after the start of the nineteenth century. So the promotion of Confucianism and Shushigaku by the bakufu and the han was a phenomenon that only suddenly came to the fore towards the closing years of the system of government established by the bakufu.

Furthermore, it is by no means the case that the bakufu sought to deny the legitimacy of other forms of learning. Kokugaku, the study of the native Japanese classics, and Rangaku, studies of the West and particularly of Dutch medicine, were permitted by the bakufu so long as their practitioners did not indulge in criticism of the bakufu. Some han even gave these and other branches of learning positive encouragement and support. Thus it would appear that Japanese learning in the Edo period was characterised by three different orientations, towards Japan itself, towards China for Confucianism and the Chinese classics, and towards the West.

The introduction of Confucianism to Japan, however, antedates the start of the Edo period by more than one thousand years. It dates back in fact to the fourth or fifth century when the Confucian classics were brought from China to Japan along with other works written in the Chinese language. Confucianism thus entered Japan through

the medium of Chinese Language and was received as a philosophy that was remote from
reality.

Confucianism rapidly became a subject for
study among the aristocrats and clergy of sixth
century Japan. For a while from the seventh century onwards, Confucianism was even made an
essential part of the education required under the
ancient bureaucratic system, following the pattern
that had earlier been established in China. But in
the middle ages, after the turn of the millenium,
Confucianism continued to be regarded not so
much as a philosophy but as a branch of learning
or study for intellectuals. It was more a matter of
Confucian study than of Confucianism as such.

In China, the land where it had originated, Confucianism naturally underwent many developments and changes and in the course of its history a number of sects or schools of thought
grew up. In time these schools of thought were
introduced to Japan too and exerted infuence on
the Confucian academic world in Japan. It was
one of these schools, Shushigaku, that was
adopted by the bakufu at the beginning of the
Edo period.

To adopt Confucianism as a practical political
philosophy was quite a different proposition from
simply taking it as a subject of purely intellectual
interest and study. As a philosophy that had been
born and grown to maturity in China, Confucianism inevitably presented a number of problems
when attempts were made to apply it to Japan,
for conditions in Japan were quite different from
those of ancient or contemporary China. Perhaps
it is not going too far to say that the differences
between the two societies were too great for
ordinary Japanese to be able to understand Con-

fucianism or put it into practice. There were also a number of areas where Confucian theory and Japanese practice were in conflict, and these posed serious problems for professional Confucian scholars.

Nevertheless, the vocabulary of Confucianism did spread throughout Japan during the Edo period, and it is still used on many occasions today. But this alone does not justify the belief that Japan has been confucianized, for this vocabulary has circulated in Japan with very different meanings from those it originally had. It is argued that Confucianism permeated throughout Japanese society in the Edo period and it would certainly be wrong to say that the Japanese have had no contact with Confucianism. But it may be truer to say that the Japanese became accustomed to using Confucian words arbitrarily in order to designate common beliefs that had long been held and that were substantially different from those of Confucianism, and in becoming so accustomed became themselves convinced that their society had been confucianized.

Marxism-Leninism has now been imported into China, the home of Confucianism, and translated into Chinese. It is said that the Chinese characters used in the translations have not been able to divest themselves of the meanings they have acquired over thousands of years and that constitute a barrier to the understanding of Marxist-Leninist thought in China. This kind of process is exactly the opposite of what happened in Japan, where imported vocabulary was used to describe native phenomena.

MORIYA-Takeshi

Land Development

During the seventeenth century the bakufu and the 'han', or feudal domains, devoted a great deal of attention to increasing the production of rice. In view of the facts that the value of land was expressed in terms of its rice-yield and that taxes were paid in rice, increasing rice production was more than just a simple matter of guaranteeing a source of food supplies. For the bakufu and the han, which could syphon off any increases through the taxation system, increases in rice production meant increases in disposable surplus rice - that is to say, increases in disposable cash income, once the rice had been turned into cash.

Efforts made to increase rice production did in fact bear fruit. It is estimated that the amount of rice produced at the end of the seventeenth century was one and a half times as much as that produced at the beginning of the century when the Edo period began, and almost twice as much by the eighteenth century.

These increases in rice production were mostly brought about by increasing the amount of land devoted to rice cultivation - by developing new paddy fields. So after the middle of the eighteenth century, when the limits of land development had been reached, growth in rice production almost came to a standstill, although there was of course some progress with land development for use as dry fields. It is clear, at any rate, that the Edo period was one in which the Japanese lands underwent a great deal of development.

Development of new paddy fields was carried out on various scales. There was small scale development of pieces of uncultivated land left around the edges of paddies that were already under cultivation, and there was large scale development involving the clearing and reclamation of tracts of wild land or marshy land that had never been cultivated. Sometimes development was carried out at the initiative of the han or the bakufu itself, while at other times it was at the initiative of local villagers, but in the case of the larger projects it often happened that merchants with sufficient capital were involved as independent contractors. Near Osaka there is a place called 'Konoike shinden' ('shinden' means 'new paddy field'). The area is now a residential district, but it used to be a famous example of land development, and Konoike is the name of the powerful city merchant who undertook the project. The area amounts to some 119 hectares and its productive capacity was assessed by the bakufu at 870 koku of rice (4437 US bushels).

One method of development commonly used during this period was that of turning the flat lands around the mouths of rivers into paddy fields. The creation of paddy fields in such places requires a high level of engineering technology on a large scale in order to prevent flooding, and for this reason such areas of land had for long remained untouched. The fact that they did eventually become targets for development shows how strong was the desire to increase the area open to rice cultivation, and success in these endeavours enabled rice production to increase considerably. Nowadays rice paddies are found by most river-mouths, and many main rice production areas are found in the vicinity of estuaries. But in most cases these are new paddies which were only developed during the Edo period, and it is these new paddies which are currently providing Japanese with most of the rice they eat.

It would of course be wrong to suppose that land development in the Edo period was confined to the development of new rice fields, for throughout the period development was taking place in Japan in various forms. On the coasts of the inland seas of Japan, for example, salt fields were established for the production of salt from the sea. The salt fields along the Inland Sea to the south of Osaka thus provided Japan with ninety per cent of its salt during the Edo period. Salt production then involved the use of sand dunes, and so it is likely that salt farming drastically altered the coastline in areas where it was practiced.

Also, in the mountains of western Japan, tree planting was carried out on a large scale, and the use of mountain and forest resources underwent considerable development. The growth of the cities, after all, created a need for the supply of large amounts of timber for building. The percentage of forest land in Japan is currently very high, but little of it is natural forest. Most is in fact the result of projects carried out in the Edo period which involved the clearing of miscellaneous woodlands and the planting of cedar and cypress trees for the lumber industry.

Useful plants such as the wax tree (Rhus silvestris), tea, and the paper mulberry were cultivated too. Cultivation developed hand in hand with local industry, as the wax trees were used to make wax, the tea plants to produce tea and the paper mulberry to make paper. Cottage industries and land development thus made much progress in mountain villages during the Edo period.

There was also a great deal of urban development in the Edo period too, for at the beginning of the sixteenth century each han set about the construction of a castle town. And the spread of the urban areas during the late seventeenth and early eighteenth centuries is also worthy of note as an instance of planned development. In the case of Kyoto, for example, during this period the city temples were moved to the outskirts, allowing redevelopment of the centre of the city, while new suburbs were developed in the areas to which the temples had moved. As these new suburbs gathered in popularity, they served to soak up some of the population of the city.

Thus throughout the Edo period there was parallel development in the farms, the mountain villages, the coastal areas and the cities. These developments changed the geographical aspect of Japan and they also made an important contribution to the development of a mature internal economy.

MORIYA-Takeshi

'Waju' (ring levee) village at intersection between Kiso River and Nagara River.

⌡ Industry

Japanese economic growth in the pre-modern era cannot be ignored in discussing today's rapid industrial development. The basis for emergence as one of the great industrial powers had been forming steadily in the pre-modern era, especially in the 18th century.

Obviously pre-modern industry was a precursor of the industrial revolution, and rested on local agriculture and forestry entirely dependent on manual labour and tools. Such industry originated from home industries, which emerged in the Kinki District in the Middle Ages spread nationwide in the 18th century, and developed into factory-style establishments at the beginning of the 19th century.

High-rise apartment house construction site (Kyodo)

Promotion of home industry resulted from not only capital investment by merchants, but also from the guidance and assistance of the local governments-han. Many of them, being in financial difficulties, attempted to increase their income by initiating new industries in their domains. Some monopolized certain products and obtained all sales profits incurred. This resulted in confrontation between han and manufacturers, often causing rebellions.

Some scholars point out governmental participation in the industrial movement as a chief feature of the Japanese political system. However, this tendency is not new.

The industrial development was deeply related to rural occupations. It was not simply confined to labour. Agricultural villages in the pre-modern era yielded wax trees, lacquer trees, tea, paper mulberry and rapeseeds, as well as foodstuff. These were so-called merchandise agriculture, the industrial raw materials were processed into lacquer, tea, paper and kerosene.

This production and processing system was particularly distinctive in mountainous regions originally unsuitable for rice cultivation. These regions could quickly respond to industrialization, owing to their flexibility with regard to rice cultivation. Besides, transport networks and transport routes were developed nationwide, closely linking urban consumers with remote rural producers.

In this respect, coastal regions were similar to mountainous ones. On barren seashores, salt fields were opened and the salt-manufacturing industry was initiated. The domestic industry of processing unedible fish into fertilizers also developed there. The coastal regions produced tiles, lacquer ware and ceramics, taking advantage of convenience to marine transport.

As indicated by these categories, pre-modern industry featured the production of basic commodities.

Almost all through the pre-modern era, trade with foreign countries was extremely limited because of the seclusion policy. Therefore, pre-modern industry was developed not by the expansion of overseas markets, but by the increase in domestic demands.

Domestic demands were supported by public consumption, mainly urban people. Pre-modern cities could not have been developed without the supply of large quantities of diverse materials commensurate with the size of the large urban consumer population. The Accumulation of the population, accompanied by urban prosperity, further increased demands for quantity and diversity of materials. This was the driving force behind the industrial development.

Thus pre-modern industry was an outgrowth of the artisan tradition from which it soon departed. From ancient times, many artisans had resided in Kyoto and Nara to provide high quality products for the nobles and to the temples. Some had fine studios and specialized in their work. Not a few operated on a scale commensurate with that of a small factory industry. These artisans usually produced a single highly skilled article for a special customer. However, pre-modern domestic industry developed in a completely opposite direction.

Take textiles for instance: Up until today, Kyoto has been a manufacturer of high class silk textiles (known as Nishijin textiles). However in the 18th century, some local regions began to manufacture slightly inferior but cheap silk textiles. Accordingly, the status of Kyoto in the silk textile industry declined relatively sharply. With the initial manufacture of cheaper cotton textiles, the textile industry immediately switched to cotton manufacture.

This is only one example. In other fields, pre--modern industry as a whole developed in response to the movement of public consumer trends.

This feature of the pre-modern industry lingered even after the markets expanded overseas following the opening of the country, the industrial revolution, and the development of heavy industry. Even today, much importance is placed on life-style-related industries, reflecting the public consumption-oriented society of Japan.

MORIYA-Takeshi

The Growth of the Bourgeoisie

Japanese cities are divided up into lots of 'cho', each 'cho' being an area rather than a street. In Europe and North America an address usually consists of the number of the house, the name of the street, and the name of the city, but in Japan, by contrast, an address consists of the number of the house, the name of the 'cho', and the name of the city. So the 'cho' is the basic unit making up the Japanese city.

Conditions are rather different now, but originally a 'cho' was a city block consisting of all the houses on both sides of a street for a part of its length - as a measure of distance the word 'cho' stands for a unit that is equivalent to one hundred and nine metres, and it was this unit that was used to divide up the streets into 'cho'. The streets of the cities were therefore endless strings of 'cho', like bead-necklaces. A 'cho' of average size had about twenty houses on each side of the street, making a total of about forty. Each 'cho' formed a neighbourhood community in which people's lives and livelihoods were shared, but they were more than that, for they had self-governing neighbourhood associations and were recognized by the civil authorities as the unit of urban administration. In the case of the large cities, a number of 'cho' would sometimes club together to form a larger unit with a larger administrative organisation.

Even in modern Japanese cities, the 'cho' is more than just part of one's address. Under some name or other, there is a self-governing association to be found in each 'cho', and they have important roles to play, not only in encouraging friendly relations among the inhabitants of the 'cho' but also in acting as the grass roots of urban administration.

'Cho' of the kind that has been described above were already in existence in Kyoto by the end of the fifteenth century, and shortly thereafter they appeared in other large cities of western Japan, such as Osaka and Sakai. They only spread over the whole country, however, after the beginning of the Edo period, in the seventeenth century.

During the Edo period the artisans and merchants living in the 'cho' were known as 'chonin', or 'cho-people', and together they constituted a new social class. Strictly speaking, of course, the word 'chonin' referred to people who not only lived in a given 'cho' but also owned their own home there. People who were 'chonin' in this sense had the right to take part in the running of the 'cho' and also had various obligations as well. In general terms, however, the expression 'chonin society' is used to refer to the society of the artisans and merchants living in the towns and cities of Japan.

There were great differences between the 'chonin' society of the seventeenth century and that of the eighteenth and nineteenth centuries. The early seventeenth century was the age of the great merchants of Osaka and Kyoto. They were full of enterprise and amassed vast sums through their willingness to take risks in such ventures as overseas trade, mining, and engineering. They were the leaders of chonin society in the cultural sphere as well, for their financial power made a certain measure of opulence and extravagance well within their command. But after the middle of the seventeenth century a large number of these merchant princes fell upon hard times. The decision by the bakufu to adopt a policy of national isolation was partly responsible for this, for it put an end to their foreign trade activities. Furthermore, official cancellations of debts to daimyos entailed great losses for the rich merchants who had lent to them.

After the fall of the merchant princes, it was the turn for the ordinary urban chonin to take centre stage of chonin society, the chonin who were characterised not by their wealth but by their frugality and willingness to work hard. And they were to be found not only in Osaka and Kyoto but also in Edo. They are also found in the novels of Ihara Saikaku, a novelist of Osaka who described the rise of the chonin class as a whole in a number of his works. This rising chonin class consisted of merchants and artisans who dealt with the goods and commodities of everyday life. The customers on whose patronage they depended were not simply a handful of individuals but the whole chonin class to which they themselves belonged, and their livelihoods were assured by the growing affluence that had been brought to urban life by the growth of the cities and the accumulation of wealth. What is more, patterns of work in the cities were such as to allow for the development of leisure time.

The accumulation of wealth, the spread of consumer habits and the growth of leisure are all held to be developments paving the way for the emergence of mass society. It would seem, therefore, that Japanese cities had some of the elements of mass society as early as the eighteenth century. Similarly, the spread of leisure activities and entertainments of various kinds, the

flourishing theatrical world, and the thriving publishing industry were not so much the products of chonin culture that they are usually taken to be but signs of the emergence of a mass culture. They would have been inconceivable without the existence of urban masses able to take part in leisure activities, indulge in theatre-going or read books. So it is surely not going too far to say that chonin society was the source from which modern Japanese urban culture and society have sprung.

MORIYA-Takeshi

1 Osaka

The three most important cities in Japan during the Edo period were Edo (now Tokyo), Kyoto and Osaka. In terms of population, Edo was the largest, with over one million, while Osaka and Kyoto both had populations of between four and five hundred thousand. All three of them were under the direct administrative control of the bakufu itself.

These three cities were referred to in the Edo period as the 'santo', an expression suggesting that they were considered the three capitals of Japan. It also shows that they were regarded as being the foremost cities in Japan at the time. Of the three, Edo was the political centre as it was the seat of the bakufu and Kyoto was the city of traditional culture as it was the home of the emperor and his court, while Osaka was a city that had been shaped by economic activity and so was sometimes even described as the 'kitchen of Japan'.

Well over a thousand years ago Osaka had been the site of a number of temporary royal capitals, but the modern city dates back to the sixteenth century when the Ishiyama Honganji temple was built there. The settlement established around the temple by its adherents rapidly grew into a substantial town. The power of the Honganji and its adherents was such that they were able to offer fierce resistance to the powerful daimyo who were trying to unify the country. Towards the end of the sixteenth century they struggled for ten years against one of these daimyo, Oda Nobunaga, but lost and were finally forced to leave Osaka. The flourishing town was reduced to ashes and ruins.

The town came to life again under Nobunaga's successor, Toyotomi Hideyoshi. Hideyoshi constructed a mighty castle on the site that had been occupied by the Honganji and he made it the administrative centre of the whole country, which he now had firmly under his control. He also arranged for the construction of a town around the castle walls and encouraged its economic growth by inviting merchants from Sakai and other towns in the vicinity.

However, after Hideyoshi's death, control of the country passed to Tokugawa Ieyasu in Edo, and after Ieyasu had become shogun and established a bakufu government, many of his opponents congregated in and around Osaka. So in the early part of the seventeenth century Ieyasu launched two attacks against Osaka castle. These resulted in the destruction of the castle and left the town in ruins once again. After this, however, the bakufu decided to rebuild Osaka. Once more the emphasis was placed on the city's economic activities and merchants from surrounding towns were encouraged to settle there. The bakufu's interest in Osaka was without doubt a product of its convenient proximity to major land and sea routes and its potential role as the economic nerve-centre of the whole country. Hideyoshi's choice of Osaka had been based on similar considerations, and it was the same circumstances that had enabled Honganji to become so powerful in the previous century.

All the 'han' set about constructing storehouses in Osaka. By the end of the seventeenth century there were one hundred of them, and in the eighteenth century, when the city reached the peak of its prosperity, more than five hundred of them lined the streets of Osaka. Each han gathered into its storehouse the rice and other products it had received in payment of taxes from the inhabitants of its domain and converted them into cash by selling when the market was right. It was to a large extent because so much of the produce of the country found its way to Osaka that the city was able to achieve the economic growth it did during the Edo period.

Popularly, Edo is known as the city of 808 districts, Kyoto as the city of 808 temples, and Osaka as the city of 808 bridges. From these expressions it would appear that Edo is renowned for its size and Kyoto and Osaka for the numbers of their temples and bridges respectively, but the bridges in Osaka's case mostly cross the canals that divide the city up in a grid-like pattern. Much of the effort that was spent in the seventeenth century on equipping Osaka for its role as a major city

Around Dojima, Osaka

was in fact devoted to the creation of a canal system, making use of the rivers that already flowed in and out of Osaka. At that time the most convenient way of transporting large quantities of goods was by ship, and the existence of a canal system made it possible for sea-going ships to make their way right into the centre of the city. The development of the canal system is therefore a token of the quantities of produce and merchandise that were being taken in and out of Osaka: at one stage it was even called the 'city of water'.

The commercial development of Osaka also exerted a considerable influence on the farming villages in the surrounding districts. Handicrafts and home industries thrived in these villages, particularly, from the eighteenth century onwards, the manufacture and processing of cotton goods.

In modern times the textile industry saw that Osaka developed from a commercial city into an industrial one. It changed from being the 'city of water' to being 'the city of smoke', and it was even called the Manchester of the East.

The concentration of urban functions in Tokyo, however, has led to a situation where it was easy to see that Osaka has declined not only in political importance but also in economic and cultural importance. So now, with its sights set on the twenty-first century, the city is planning a new role for itself.

MORIYA-Takeshi

1 National Isolation

For more than two centuries, from the beginning of the seventeenth century until the middle
of the nineteenth century, Japan was in a state of
isolation from all foreign countries. The reason
for this was that the bakufu was pursuing a policy
of forbidding the nation free contact with foreign
countries. This policy, or state of affairs, is given
the name 'sakoku'.

Curiously enough, Japan was not the only
country to be pursuing such a policy at this time.
It is important to remember that a number of
other countries in east Asia, including of course
Ch'ing China, were in a state of sakoku, or something similar to it, at the same time. Sakoku was
in fact the negative form which the international
order in east Asia had taken at that time.

Until just before the start of the isolation entailed by the sakoku policy, the Japanese people
had been experiencing a period of internationa-
lisation, a kind of period rarely met with in
Japanese history. In the middle of the sixteenth
century, some Portuguese ships drifted ashore at
Tanegashima Island to the south of Kyushu and
introduced European-style guns to Japan. Subsequently the Spanish missionary Francis Xavier
came to Japan, and the work of preaching Christianity in Japan began. The tide of the era of the
great European voyages of exploration had finally
reached Far Eastern shores, and this meant for
Japanese their first contacts with the material and
spiritual civilisations of the West.

Japanese armed merchantmen had already
been active in the East China Sea, but now, under
the stimulus of the Portuguese and Spanish trad-

ers, they made advances into South-East Asia and in various places established Japanese townships. By the beginning of the seventeenth century, there are said to have been more than five thousand Japanese living abroad in these townships. If the bakufu had not introduced the policy of sakoku, there might well have been in the middle of the seventeenth century a decisive confrontation, perhaps in the Bay of Bengal, between a Japan advancing from the Far East towards South-East Asia and the European countries, especially England, which were extending their administration over eastern India. But owing to the sakoku policy, of course, such a confrontation did not take place, and what is more, the Japanese residents in the various overseas Japanese communities were unable to return home to Japan and were abandoned where they were.

The propagation of Christianity in Japan reached heights that are hard to imagine. It is said that during the first twenty years of missionary work more than two hundred churches were built throughout western Japan, and that in less than half a century the number of believers had reached several hundred thousand. But as the internal disturbances of the end of the sixteenth century were coming to an end and a new social structure was being established, the existence of the foreign missionaries and the propagation of Christianity began to be something of an incovenience for the rulers of Japan. So up until the year 1687 there were repeated deportations of missionaries from Japan and repeated incidents of the oppression of believers. The problems associated with Christianity at this time were one of the reasons for the sakoku policy.

The sakoku policy was brought into effect at the beginning of the Edo period by means of a mass of legal ordinances. These included the prohibition of Christianity, the prohibition of voyages overseas undertaken by Japanese, restrictions on foreign trade, and so on, and they were enacted during the course of the 1630s. Meanwhile, in 1637 there was a large-scale Christian rebellion in Kyushu. It thus appears that the development of the sakoku policy was a result of the anti-Christian stance adopted by the bakufu, which was much afraid of the infiltration of Christianity into Japan. But on the other hand there was also the desire of the Netherlands to exclude all other countries from contact with Japan and to develop a trade monopoly with Japan. The Netherlands were late to join the Far East trade compared with Portugal and Spain and, being a Protestant country while Spain and Portugal were Catholic, did not seek from Japan permission to preach Christianity in return for trade. At heart the bakufu did have an aversion to Christianity, but it did not want to abandon the profits to be had from trade. Therefore the Netherlands were a suitable country with which to carry on trade. During the years of sakoku, the bakufu determined that the only countries to have trade contacts with Japan were to be the Netherlands and also China, which had had nothing to do with the proselytisation of Christianity at all.

The bakufu had also for some time been thinking of making foreign trade a bakufu monopoly. This was because the bakufu knew that many daimyo in western Japan had been actively engaging in foreign trade and securing considerable profits. In order for the bakufu to keep all these profits under its control, it was necessary to place a total ban on free foreign trade. This also had the effect of preventing the daimyo of western Japan from enriching themselves beyond the bakufu's wishes. During the sakoku period the bakufu established Nagasaki in Kyushu as its commercial port, and there only a group of privileged merchants was allowed to continue trading with the Netherlands and China.

In sum, the sakoku policy was adopted in order to eliminate Christianity and to secure for the bakufu a monopoly of trade profits. Thus the term sakoku is one that refers to the results, and it is altogether another question whether the bakufu intended from the start to shut off the country completely or not. It is difficult to deny, however, that as a result of the sakoku policy the Japanese lost interest in foreign countries and gradually developed an insular national character.

But while there were those demerits of the sakoku policy, it is also the case that during the two hundred years of sakoku the domestic natural resources of Japan were developed, a domestic economy grew to maturity, and the nation attained prosperity and acquired technological skills. It was during this period too that Japanese traditional culture, style of life and values were formed. And Japan was never subject to colonial rule!

In the year 1853 Commodore Perry's fleet of 'Black Ships' arrived in Tokyo Bay and sought trade between Japan and America. This was the opportunity that led to sakoku being abandoned, and less than twenty years later the Edo bakufu itself had collapsed.

MORIYA-Takeshi

Nagasaki, a Window on the World

Throughout the greater part of the Edo period, Japan was isolated from the rest of the world. This does not mean, however, that Japan had no contact whatsoever with the outside world. The bakufu made Nagasaki in Kyushu its one trading port and maintained some of its trading activities, albeit only with China and Holland.

Nagasaki had been a focal point for trade with the so-called 'southern barbarians', meaning mainly the Europeans, since the sixteenth century. Its links with various European coutries were close, and at the end of the sixteenth century it even happened that the local daimyo gave the town to the Jesuits for a while for use as their own territory. This gift of land to the Jesuits excited fears among some of the leaders of Japan at the time that the Christian countries might be hoping to make some territorial gains in Japan, and it was one of the factors that led Japan to adopt a policy of national isolation.

Nagasaki came under the direct jurisdiction of the bakufu itself, and a bakufu official was appointed to look after the administration of the city. It served as the home base for the 'licensed ships' carrying on trade with South-East Asia, but once the isolation policy had been adopted it acquired a lasting monopoly not only of trade but also of information from the Western world. It may have been Japan's only window on the world but in terms of the effect it had on Japan, it can be said to have functioned quite efficiently.

Of all the European countries it was Holland

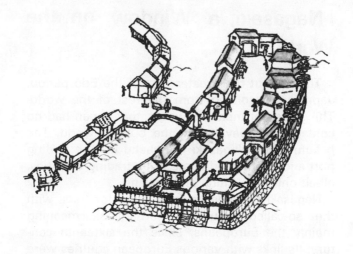

Deshima-Fold screens of Nagasaki (Stored by Nagasaki Municipal Museum)

that had the monopoly of trade with Japan. On the island of Deshima in Nagasaki the Dutch had their own trading station. Ordinary Japanese were not allowed on the island, and the Dutchmen working at the station were required to live on the island and their lives were subject to a number of restrictions. Nevertheless, the fact that people from a foreign country were in residence there affected the city as a whole in various ways, and even now Nagasaki has a unique atmosphere that has a touch of something foreign about it. Special officials were appointed by the bakufu to deal with the Dutchmen on Deshima and by the middle of the nineteenth century there were about one hundred and forty of them. Quite a number of them would have had a fair degree of competence in Dutch. In modern terms, these officials combined the duties of interpreters and customs officials and they comprised most of the small number of Japanese who were allowed to come into direct contact with the Dutch. Through their contacts with the Dutch, some of them came to acquire a considerable amount of knowledge about the West, and especially to learn about the natural sciences. These men had an important role to play in the development of the school of learning known as 'rangaku', or Dutch studies, which took its place alongside the pre-existing schools of study that concentrated on Japan or China.

In these circumstances it was inevitable that those who wished to acquire some knowledge of Western learning should make their way to Nagasaki and pursue their studies there. Nagasaki therefore became the home of Western learning in Japan. At the same time, the Dutch were required, in return for their monopoly on the Japan trade, to keep the bakufu informed on a wide range of subjects. The information they provided was swiftly translated by bakufu officials and forwarded to Edo. These reports gave the bakufu some knowledge of current affairs throughout the world. It was in this way that the bakufu was able to learn about Commodore Perry's expedition to Japan in the 1850s before his arrival.

The eagerness with which the bakufu sought information on the West and on Western learning is also apparent from the trade conducted through Nagasaki: amongst the items imported into Japan were books as well as cotton and medical supplies. In the second half of the eighteenth century the bakufu made special efforts to have more books brought into the country, and these in turn raised the level of interest in Japan in medicine, the natural sciences and other branches of contemporary European learning. In the nineteenth century the bakufu even set up a translation centre in Edo, where scholars who could read Dutch were set to work translating books in Dutch.

Apart from the merchants who handled the trade, there were also Dutch doctors and scientists living on Deshima. The names of two of them, Kaempfer and Siebold, are well known to Japanese even today. Their infuence on contemporary Japanese intellectuals was naturally great, but it should not be forgotten that they also applied their powers of scientific observation to Japan and wrote books based on what they had observed. Thus at the same time as conveying information about the West to Japan, they also told Europeans about Japan and pioneered the study of Japan in the West. In this sense Nagasaki was not only a window on the world for Japan but also a window on Japan for the world.

MORIYA-Takeshi

Leisure

It is recorded that a certain foreigner who was travelling in Japan in the nineteenth century was quite astonished to find how enthusiastic the urban inhabitants of Edo were about caring for plants and flowers. He was surprised because the care of plants seemed to him to be the kind of occupation that in Japan only aristocrats would indulge in. But in Edo, even the people who lived in tenement buildings took pleasure in looking after plants—it was a very ordinary hobby commonly enjoyed by a large percentage of the inhabitants of the city. The cultivation of the morning glory was particularly popular and many people were experimenting with the cross-fertilization of different varieties in the hope of producing a new

Plant Market in Asakusa, Tokyo

variety with curious features of its own. In Europe it was in the nineteenth century that Mendel worked out the principles of heredity, but commoners of Edo, like those of Europe, already were familiar with the basic principles of plant heredity through their experiments with plants of all kinds.

The culture of the urban dwellers of the Edo period ranged from painting to the theatre and in each field the work of outstanding artists and specialists raised the standards of cultural activity. But the other side of cultural life in the Edo period, the involvement of amateurs in hobbies of all kinds, should not be forgotten. Some of the hobbies or interests enjoyed by the common people of Edo, such as higher mathematics, seem today to be more suitable as objects of scientific or academic study, and they would perhaps have seemed so to visiting foreigners in the nineteenth century, too. However, little thought was given to applying the knowledge thus gained, for example to use the knowledge gained from plant breeding to crop production. Instead, efforts were concentrated solely on producing unusual varieties of the morning glory. Similarly, when a difficult mathematical problem had been solved, no thought was given to making use of it in such fields as engineering, and all that was done was to offer the solution to the gods in a shrine. Thus when an area of interest became taken up as a hobby, it remained to the last a pure hobby.

From the middle of the nineteenth century onwards the Japanese came into contact with the West again. Japanese showed no bewilderment when faced with Western science or learning, but rather welcomed its introduction to Japan. One of the explanations for the ease with which Western learning was able to permeate Japan may well be the experience of accumulating knowledge by means of hobbies throughout the Edo period. It is also true that the bakufu allowed the pursuit of foreign learning (Rangaku) as long as it did not threaten the social system.

In the Edo period all popular hobbies had one feature in common, and that was the importance of the element of 'practice' or 'training'. The acquisition of technological skills, of knowledge, or of such social accomplishments as the tea ceremony could all become hobbies so long as one acquired them from the right sort of teacher. The concept of 'training' implied a lack of any practical objective in learning and, unimaginable though it is to us today, even medicine could become a subject for training and learning for its own sake. Of course, it was not the case that the knowledge acquired through a given hobby was intrinsically useless, but it was regarded as a misfortune to have to rely on that knowledge in order to make a living, and it was thought that the ideal was 'training' for the sake of 'training'.

Such traditional Japanese arts as the tea ceremony and the art of flower arrangement were originally enjoyed only by special classes of people with the leisure for such pursuits, but once these arts had been popularized, 'training' in the skills and knowledge required became popular throughout Japan as hobbies for people of all classes. It was in connection with this growing popularity that during the Edo period the 'iemoto' system developed whereby particular families of specialists controlled the 'training' offered in a given hobby or cultural pursuit.

Towards the end of the seventeenth century guide-books were published for all the cities in Japan. These guide-books contained lists of the scholars and artists living in each city. To prevent misunderstanding it should be mentioned here that not all the men whose names appeared in the guide-books were in fact experts in the fields they professed. They were all, however, people who were making their living by offering 'training' in one skill or another to the common people. Within the network embracing the 'iemoto' house and the ordinary people taking up the hobbies for themselves, these teachers played the role of mediators between the specialists who were the nucleus of the 'iemoto' system and the hordes of amateurs who were seeking 'training'.

The end of the seventeenth century corresponds with the period in which the culture of the townsmen was gradually taking shape in the cities, and the lists in the guide-books suggest that various forms of 'training' had an important part to play in the formation of that culture. They also suggest that there are cultural links between the end of the seventeenth century and the present day, for now hobby schools and culture centres enjoy great popularity in Japan's cities and offer a variety of courses. Japanese today naturally enjoy such activities as tennis or handicrafts, but they are at the same time quite happy for such activities to become purely a matter of 'training', and it would seem that the passionate pursuit of 'training' in a hobby, which was so common during the Edo period, is now returning to Japan.

MORIYA-Takeshi

Travelling

Towards the end of the seventeenth century a German doctor came to Japan and travelled from Nagasaki in Kyushu to Edo (now Tokyo). He recorded that he was much impressed by the excellent facilities provided for the traveller along the way, including overnight accommodation; that anybody could travel without danger since the authorities made a good job of preserving the public peace; and that enormous numbers of people were taking advantage of the good conditions for travelling prevailing in Japan and could be seen travelling up and down the highways. It is doubtful that he would have been so impressed with the state of things in Japan if conditions had been more or less the same in his own country.

Travel was also a characteristic of the Middle Ages preceding the Edo period. There were large numbers of entertainers and peddlers, who earned their living while travelling constantly on the road between towns and farming villages. There were also many literary figures who kept themselves aloof from the everyday world and found in travel the essence that made life worth living for them. One would also have seen people whose religion had led them to take to the road, either to undertake the work of proselytizers or to make a pilgrimage to some sacred place.

The repertory of the Noh theatre, the classical theatre of Japan which developed in the fourteenth century, contains many plays concerning travel. In many of the plays a priest or monk on a pilgrimage stops at a village on the way and has a strange experience. Examples such as this serve to reinforce the impression that the Middle Ages were a time of travel in Japan.

With the start of the Edo period in the seventeenth century, however, the people who in previous centuries had made a living from travel were forced by the authorities to take up settled residence somewhere. Japanese society in the Edo period was one which required, at least in principle, everybody to have a social status, a place of residence and a fixed occupation. So if one looks at life in the Edo period in the light of the principles according to which society was organized, it does appear to be a rigid society: one that was very far from being in a state of flux. It is true that nomadic ways of life did come to an end and that a certain amount of social stability was achieved, but, ironically it is also true that the more stable society became, the more the common people became interested in travel and short-term movement about the country.

One of the factors which encouraged the common people to take to travel in the Edo period was the custom of making pilgrimages to shrines and temples. Most notable in this respect were the group pilgrimages to the famous Ise shrine in modern Mie Prefecture. Ise pilgrimages went through a resurgence of popularity every fifty or sixty years from 1650 onwards; at such times the roads were packed with people from all over the country making their way to Ise. According to surviving records, just fifty days in the popular year of 1705 saw some 3,620,000 pilgrims making their way to Ise, while in 1830 there were 2,280,000 pilgrims in one month alone. Even by today's standards, these are by no means small numbers. Since most of those taking part were not samurai but farmers or ordinary city-dwellers, it seems that there were extraordinary numbers of ordinary people making their way through the towns and countryside of Japan. It is perhaps reasonable to view these years as exceptional and to suppose that the bursts of enthusiasm for pilgrimages to Ise owed something to a kind of temporary madness, but it remains true that throughout the Edo period villages and towns were constantly choosing representatives to send on a pilgrimage to Ise or to some other famous temples or shrines. Some special pilgrimage routes became established too, such the ones around the thirty-three temples of western Japan (centering on Osaka and Kyoto) and the eighty-eight temples of Shikoku, and large numbers of people followed these routes on their pilgrimages. It was not uncommon in some areas for the experience of travel to be seen as a kind of rite of passage into adulthood.

Even in the Middle Ages there had been people who made their living by guiding travellers to their destinations, especially among religious people of low social status. By the eighteenth century there also existed agents who handled travel business of all kinds, and in the nineteenth century some Japanese inns even formed themselves into associations. The increasing numbers of travellers made it possible to earn a living from the travel business, and at the same time the increasingly well-organised facilities for travel encouraged more and more people to take to the road with the expectation of having a safe and comfortable journey.

In the Edo period there was a good network of roads and navigation routes. Of course, when the bakufu undertook to maintain a road system it had in mind mainly such forms of official travel as the regular movement of the daimyo between

Edo and their domains in the country, and it was not thinking of making things convenient for the ordinary traveller. In addition to the five official main roads radiating out of Edo, there were also large numbers of other roads, and it is these that the merchants probably used for the most part. Similarly, the navigation routes were principally developed for the transportation of tax-rice and thus for the benefit of the bakufu and the daimyo, and no thought was given to the possibility of commoners travelling by sea in a private capacity. Once the facilites for travel were there, however, whether at sea or on land, everybody made use of them. Thus the highways established by the bakufu rapidly became highways for everybody, irrespective of status, and the same was true of the navigation routes as well.

In the nineteenth century a comic novel called *Shank's Mare* dealing with the adventures of two commoners as they travelled down the Tokaido highway from Edo to Kyoto became a best seller and the famous printmaker Hiroshige made a very popular series of prints covering the fifty-three stages of the Tokaido. Thus travel by commoners became a theme of literature and art before Japan's move into the modern age.

Japanese are just as happy to travel now as they were in the Edo period and the preference of the Japanese for group travel has continued to the present-day. Tourist spots are still concentrated around shrines and temples, as before. It is also interesting to note that many of Japan's earliest local railways were constructed along the routes to famous temples and shrines such as Nikko, Ise, and Kotohira, with a view to carrying pilgrims as passengers.

MORIYA-Takeshi

₁ The Theatre

One of the main forms of mass entertainment during the Edo period was the theatre. Outings to the theatre were a regular part of life in the larger cities from the seventeenth century onwards.

The theatre first made its appearance in Japan in the Middle Ages when stages for performing Noh plays were established. This development took place during the Muromachi period (1333-1573), and the Noh theatre is thought to have set the pattern for Japanese theatres in the following centuries. In Noh theatres today, the stage and the seats for the audience all shelter under one and the same roof, but originally there were two separate buildings, one for the stage and one for the audience, and the seats sheltered by a roof were for those members of the audience who were of high rank. Between this gallery for the high-ranking and the stage itself there was an open space and it was here that the common people gathered to watch plays. This arrangement is remarkably similar to that of English theatres at the time of Shakespeare.

The principle theatrical arts of the Edo period were the kabuki theatre and the puppet theatre, or ningyō jōruri (also known as bunraku). The theatres in which performances of both were held owed much to the earlier Noh theatres in that the stage was a separate entity. Nowadays, in theatres devoted to performances of the traditional performing arts of Japan, one usually finds a stylized roof fitted above the stage as a decoration, which is a reminder of the architectural traditions connected with the theatre in Japan. Alternatively, one finds attached to the front of the balcony containing the upper level of seats something rather like the eaves of a building, which similarly serves to show that stage and audience were once under separate roofs.

During the Edo period there was in or near the centre of most cities a street full of theatres, although precise information is wanting in the case of cities that were not under the direct control of the bakufu. In Kyoto, around Shijo Kawaramachi, and in Dōtonbori in Osaka, theatres are still to be found in the areas that were traditionally set aside for theatres in the Edo period. In the case of Tokyo (Edo), however, urban development has been too rapid to leave any traces of the old theatre districts discernible today.

In these theatre districts, there were a number of grand theatres licensed by the bakufu as permanent theatres. In Edo there were three, in Osaka five, and in Kyoto there were seven at the peak. Performances were staged at these grand theatres all the year round, but there were also smaller theatres which operated for shorter periods, and the number of these was more than ten times the number of grand theatres.

There were also theatres of all sizes scattered around the country in local towns and cities. A document has survived which gives a list of these theatres as they existed at the beginning of the nineteenth century. The list is incomplete, but it nevertheless gives a total of 132 places throughout the country where theatres could be found. This makes it clear that there was in Japan in the Edo period a sizable population of people who were addicted to the pleasures of the theatre, and a population sufficient to support a surprisingly large number of theatres. During this period there were enormous numbers of books published dealing with or relating to the theatre in some way, and this was one of the special features of the publishing world at that time, but it is also clear that behind this publishing activity was the support of a vast population interested in the theatre.

In the streets where the grand theatres were offering entertainment throughout the year, there were also a large number of other entertainment facilities. Foremost amongst them were places where food or drink could be had, but there were also shops selling trinkets and souvenirs, amusement halls, and misemono-goya (exhibition tents for freaks and other side-shows). If you replace the misemono-goya with cinemas, the scene differs very little from the entertainment areas in Japan's modern cities. In fact, it can be said that the style of these entertainment areas was established by the theatre districts in the Edo period.

There were also in the theatre districts a number of restaurants which had special contracts with the theatres. Here you could book tickets for performances, purchase programmes, rest during the intervals, and you could order from these restaurants food and drink to be brought to you in your place in the theatre. They thus provided all the services that a theatregoer could possibly find himself in need of, and so they were much patronized by the richer members of the audiences. Of course those sitting in the ordinary seats - although in the Edo period the entire audience sat not on chairs but on mats in small compartments - did not need to make bookings beforehand and all they had to do was buy their tickets at the door as they went in.

The large theatres had their own actors, who were bound to them by contracts that were renewable at the end of each year. These actors had their own homes near the theatres and commuted to the theatres they were contracted to play for. They did not set out so much to please particular members of the audience as to act and leave the audience to evaluate their acting skills. All they had to do, in other words, was to sell their skills like any other commercial product. If they proved popular with their audiences, then they could demand a more lucrative contract for the following year. Thus the actors were not simply hirelings of the theatres - they did have a certain amount of independence as well. In the past in most countries, performing artists of all kinds led unsettled and insecure lives on the fringes of society, or a servile existence attached to some patron or other. Even in the contemporary world there are still performing artists in some countries who find themselves in one or other of these situations. In the Edo period, such actors were common of course, and it cannot be argued that they do not exist in Japan today. Nevertheless a number of actors in the Edo period enjoyed a settled and independent existence as actors under contract to particular theatres. And their livelihoods were guaranteed by the phenomenon in Japan of the theatre districts, which provided many opportunities for employment.

MORIYA-Takeshi

Books and Publishing

During the Edo period an extraordinarily large number of popular publications were produced for the mass-market. This fact provides some indication of the high level of literacy obtaining in Japan at the time.

Many different kinds of publication were developed in Japan during the Edo period, including 'kawaraban', which were simple news-sheets, 'banzuke', which were lists of things in order of priority (such as kinds of cake, famous wrestlers, and so on), and the delicate wood-block prints known as 'ukiyo-e'. These signalled the emergence of a culture of the printed word. Such developments were based on the publication of items that appealed to popular tastes and needs.

An examination of the publishing world of Edo reveals that at first most publications were Japanese and Chinese classics and Buddhist works. At this stage publication was a business aimed at the intellectuals, principally scholars, priests and doctors. But a turning-point came at the end of the seventeenth century when changes took place which led to a great expansion of the potential and expected readership of books. There was a marked tendency for the best-sellers to be of light-weight subjects such as works which took their subject matter from the tastes and manners of the contemporary world, the guide-books to the cities, easy educational works, books on various hobbies and amusements, and pornography too; meanwhile the weightier works, such as the classics and Buddhist works, came to be less and less the main concern of the publishing industry. Even with Buddhist publications, it was not the original scriptures that were now popular so much as the books which explained Buddhist doctrine in simple terms.

This phenomenon is clearly indicative of the fact that the purchasing and reading public no longer came solely from a narrow class of intellectuals as had been the case hitherto but now came instead from the ordinary city-dwellers. It is also indicative of the fact that the populace had developed to the point of being able and interested enough to buy, read and understand books.

Developments of this sort are reflected in the rapid growth of the publishing industry during the course of the seventeenth century. In Kyoto, which was the centre of the publishing industry, there seem to have been some seventy or eighty publishing houses at the end of the seventeenth century, and it is calculated that they were producing about one hundred and seventy new publications in an average year. During the first half of the seventeenth century the number of new publications was about thirty per year, so a comparison reveals that in the course of half a century the publishing industry had achieved a growth rate of some four hundred per cent. It is clear, then, that publishing was a growth industry during the seventeenth century, and this growth was encouraged, and the fortunes of the industry assured, by the extension of the reading public to include ordinary city dwellers.

Just before the start of the Edo period, the technique of movable-type printing was introduced to Japan from Korea. The clarity produced by this new method of printing was superior to that produced by the wood-block method, which had been in sole use hitherto in Japan, and so during the early Edo period a number of high-quality publications appeared which had been printed using the movable-type method of printing and then elegantly bound. In time however, as publishing came to concern itself with the mass market, the wood-block method came back into favour, for what it lacked in terms of clarity it made up for in its suitability for mass production. And the result was that movable-type printing, with which it was not practicable to produce more than about a hundred copies of a given work, virtually disappeared.

The wood-block method of printing also imposed its own limitations on the publishing industry, and by modern standards the number of copies printed of each work was pathetically small - usually around two to three hundred for a first edition. But this did represent something of an improvement when compared with what had been possible with movable-type printing. In the case of best-sellers, reprinting brought the number of copies up to several thousand or even as many as ten thousand, but reprinting on a scale such as this is only found well after the end of the seventeenth century.

Be that as it may, since the number of copies that could be produced of a given work was limited in this way, it was inevitable that the price per copy was by no means a cheap one by the standards of the day. But through the medium of the commercial lending libraries known as 'kashihon'ya' it was possible even for the poorer city dwellers to become acquainted with books. Some 'kashihon'ya' even took their books out to farming villages in the country on regular trips to their customers, and their role in furthering the spread of books amongst the populace was a considerable one. Their role was akin to that of the public library today, but they also handled books in

Yaesu Book Centre, Tokyo

manuscript, for during the Edo period the bakufu placed many restrictions on the activities of publishers, and books which were thought likely to be banned were simply circulated in manuscript via the 'kashihon'ya' network instead.

Publishing in Japan, of course, did not begin in the Edo period: Japan has a long tradition of printing and publishing which goes back to the earliest times. In the eighth century one million small wooden pagodas were made each containing a short passage of Buddhist scripture printed with copper plates. A number of these survive and, bar one slightly earlier example from Korea, these are the world's oldest samples of print.

The mass-market publishing industry of Japan during the Edo period was built on these old foundations. By the end of the eighteenth century it had made further progress which resulted in the development of the refined techniques used to produce the wood-block print, and it is widely known that the Impressionist painters of nineteenth-century France were much inspired by these Japanese wood-block prints.

MORIYA-Takeshi

Educating the Nation

The current Japanese literacy rate stands at very close to one hundred per cent. And it is said that the general level of mathematical ability in Japan is very high too. It is probably fair to say that these high levels of numeracy and literacy are a reflection of the skills and abilities of the Japanese as a nation.

It goes without saying, though, that these levels of ability were not achieved over a short period of time. Rather, it should be said that they are the products of decades if not centuries of popular education from the Edo period onwards.

In the Edo period education for common people was in the hands of private schools. The bakufu and the han were enthusiastic about the education of their vassals, the samurai, but they took no part in the education of the farmers or the merchant classes and gave it no particular encouragement. It was rather through the initiative of the townsmen themselves that educational institutions were established in Edo period Japan and that education spread throughout the country.

At first it was mostly Buddhist temples that provided the premises for the holding of classes, and for this reason private educational institutions came to be generally referred to as 'terakoya', a word which means 'a temple barrack'. But it was far from true that all popular education was conducted in temple compounds. In a picture showing urban Kyoto at the end of the seventeenth century a 'terakoya' school can be seen at work on the second floor of a bookshop. So it would appear that in some cases publishing, bookselling and education were conducted on the same premises. Institutions for the education of commoners like 'terakoya' had in fact existed from as early as the Muromachi period in the fifteenth century, but it was only in the Edo period, particularly from the beginning of the eighteenth century onwards, that they came to play an important role.

It is estimated that the total number of 'terakoya' founded throughout the Edo period in all parts of Japan was not less than ten thousand. There were rapid rises in their numbers after the start of the nineteenth century, with an average of 140 being established throughout the country each year during the 1830s, 240 a year during the 1840s, and more than 300 a year during the 1850s. When allowance is made for the different levels of population density, there seems to have been little difference between the provision of educational facilities in urban areas and in country areas. These figures should serve to give a good idea of just how eager the common people were for education in the Edo period. It is often pointed out that the Japanese today place a lot of importance on education, but it should be remembered that this is a phenomenon that can be traced back to the Edo period.

In passing it should be mentioned that the modern education system set up after the Meiji Restoration of 1868 at first relied to some extent on interested individuals or towns and villages to take the initiative and set up schools in their areas. The government was less of a leader than a follower. This too gives some idea of the eagerness of the Japanese for education.

But be that as it may, 'terakoya' schools in the Edo period usually consisted of just one classroom and one teacher for twenty to thirty pupils.

'Terakoya' by L. Crepon, *Le Japon Illustré* par Aimé Humberp,
Tokyo: Yushodo Bookseller Co., Ltd.

It is recorded that some 'terakoya' had as many as several hundred pupils, but schools on such a scale must be considered to have been exceptional and the basic pattern of the 'terakoya' was one room and one teacher. Thus the teacher was generally also the one who was responsible for running the school. At first villages entrusted 'terakoya' to the care of a Buddhist or Shinto priest or of a samurai not in service to a daimyo, whose livelihood depended on running the school and doing the teaching required. In some cases doctors took on the role of teacher in addition to their professional activities. But as the end of the Edo period drew closer, it became usual for commoners to take over the running of the schools and the teaching for themselves.

The education provided by the 'terakoya' concentrated on reading and writing, and in urban 'terakoya' attended by the children of merchants it was also usual to teach the children how to use the 'soroban' or abacus. Thus it is clear that from their beginnings the 'terakoya' aimed at improving the literacy and numeracy of the common people.

The teaching of reading and writing did not of course concern itself solely with the acquisition of those skills, for it was expected that the children would accumulate knowledge at the same time as they were learning to read and write what they had learnt. A variety of texts were used to provide practice in reading and writing: these materials included passages relating to geography, history, industry, science and mathematics as well as model letters, and so on. The children attending the 'terakoya' presumably absorbed the knowledge contained in the materials they were learning to read and write from.

An important aspect of 'terakoya' education was that the texts used by 'terakoya' throughout the country were generally published books, which inevitably meant that Japanese education in the Edo period contained elements of national uniformity. No matter where the 'terakoya' was and no matter who was doing the teaching, pupils throughout Japan were using more or less the same textbooks and thus receiving more or less the same kind of education. It should perhaps be added that an education system of this kind ultimately prevented the development of personal and creative education and thereby made it difficult for the abilities of all Japanese to be exercized to the full.

MORIYA-Takeshi

Black Ships from America

The expression 'black ships', in Japanese kuro-fune, originally referred to the sailing ships which reached Japan from Europe centuries ago. In a Japanese-Portuguese dictionary compiled in the early seventeenth century, the word 'curofune' as it was spelt, was defined as "a man-of-war coming from India, or ships treated with coal-tar like ocean-going sailing ships". Western ships were mostly made from oak, but because oak was particularly susceptible to woodworm, various methods had been used over the years to prevent the destruction of the timber, at first by lining the hull with lead, and later by giving the hull a coating made of a mixture of pine resin, tar, hair and pine shavings. Compared with the plain, untreated wood of Japanese sailing ships, the Western ships did in fact look black, and that is how they got their name. These black ships, loaded with the products of a distant civilization, conjured up a sense of the exotic.

Owing to the national isolation policy, however, the black ships disappeared from Japanese waters during the seventeenth century, except for the annual arrival of Dutch sailing ships at Nagasaki. The expression itself came to be forgotten in time. In the second half of the eighteenth century Western ships came to be sighted once again off the coasts of Japan from time to time, but most Japanese then did not perceive them as any kind of military threat. But in the summer of 1853, four black ships weighed anchor in what is now Tokyo Bay. Their hulls were huge and black, and two of them were belching smoke. The United States East Indies Fleet, under the command of Com-

modore Matthew Perry, had finally reached
Japan. His ships differed from the black ships of
the past - not only because some of them were
steamships but also because they constituted a
military threat. The image that the Japanese have
today of the black ships was formed in that year.
The huge steamships were the first pieces of
modern weaponry that the Japanese had seen,
and to a contemporary witness they were
"floating sea-fortresses" and speed was theirs to
command. The flagship 'Susquehanna' was a
paddle-steamer of 2450 tons, and it is now estimated that the largest sailing ships in Japan at
that time displaced a mere two hundred tons. To
call it a 'floating sea-fortress' was far from being
an exaggeration - it was rather a vivid expression
for those who saw it.

Perry's fleet succeeded in obtaining an important concession from the bakufu, an agreement to
put an end to the long period of Japanese isolation, and this was achieved without firing a single
shot, for the black ships themselves were an elo-
quent display of military might. The bakufu had
long prided itself on the absolute authority it
commanded within Japan, but when faced with
the threat posed by the black ships it was unable
even to wage a war, and its authority was dealt a
severe blow. While the black ships aroused
nationalistic emotions among the Japanese people, the bakufu sought to suppress these emotions. This repressed nationalism came to the sur-
face in the form of criticism of the Treaty of Kanagawa and the other treaties the bakufu concluded
with the Western powers in the 1850s. The issue
of whether the country should be opened to the
Westerners or not gave rise to a good deal of
political strife and disruption, and in the midst of

all the confusion, the Tokugawa bakufu finally collapsed, thus bringing feudalism in Japan to an end. It is on account of this pattern of events that most Japanese today incline to the belief that it was because of the shock caused by the black ships that modern Japan came to be born at all.

The arrival of the black ships had a great historical role to play in prompting Japanese modernization. From the last days of the bakufu up until Japan's defeat in the World War II, Japanese policy was epitomised by the expression 'Fukoku kyōhei', or 'A Rich Country and a Strong Army'. The advanced countries of the West were militarily strong, as was clearly demonstrated by the black ships alone; they had sufficient economic resources to support their military might; and behind all this was their science and technology. In order to attain equality with the advanced countries of Europe and America and to maintain Japan's independence, Japan had to acquire the military might, the industrial strength, and the science and technology that they had. So 'Fukoku kyōhei' was a slogan that was expressive of Japan's determination to catch up.

The desire to catch up depended on a finely balanced set of circumstances. The countries looked up to as models had to have reached a stage of development that was higher than that of Japan, but if the gap was too great then it would lead not to a determined attempt to catch up, rather to resignation and the abandoning of the attempt. In the middle of the nineteenth century, England, France, Germany, and the United States were one after the other becoming industrialized, but industrialization was still at an early stage. Steampower was in use, but only in a few select areas of industry, and in the wooden steamships the steam engines played only an auxiliary role. Thus the steamship 'Mississippi' took 226 days to reach Tokyo Bay after leaving Norfolk with Commodore Perry aboard. The Japanese reaction to the advent of the black ships was over-sensitive, but it prompted Japan to set out as the last runner in the nineteenth century race for industrialization.

In 1853 the black ships were not the symbols of peaceful cultural contact the earlier black ships had been; rather, they constituted an expression of military might. But for geographical reasons Japan had traditionally not placed as much importance on military might as the countries of the West. After three hundred years, during which it had made no efforts to build up its military strength, Japan suddenly started learning from the European civilizations that had produced a figure like Napoleon.

Looking back, the arrival of the black ships was a fateful meeting between a civilization that was based on military expansionism and one that was not. The period from then up to the defeat in the Pacific War, almost a hundred years, was Japan's most European period in that the linchpin of state policy was the idea of a strong army. It may be that this period will turn out to have been something of an exception in the long march of Japan's history.

SONODA-Hidehiro

Sapporo, Japan's new star in the North

Sapporo is the capital of Hokkaido, which accounts for twenty-two per cent of Japan's total land area. Hokkaido is the northernmost of Japan's four main islands and was the last frontier until modern times. The development of Hokkaido is epitomized by the growth of Sapporo, for the construction of Sapporo was only started in 1869 and yet within a hundred years it had attained a population of one million. In 1983 it overtook the ancient capital of Kyoto and became Japan's fifth largest city in terms of population. Its growth in the last fifteen years has been particularly remarkable, for its population has increased by one hundred per cent.

In two respects Sapporo differs from other Japanese cities. Firstly, there is the fact of its geographical location at latitude 43° north, which puts it on a level with Munich and Boston and gives it an average annual temperature of 8.4 degrees centigrade, whereas the average temperature of Tokyo throughout the year is 17 degrees. The average temperature during January, February and March is below freezing and lowest temperature ever recorded is minus 24 degrees. Thus the usual styles of Japanese housing, which are based on an expectation of mild winters, are of little use in Hokkaido, and the double-glazed houses with colourful roofs that abound in the suburbs of Sapporo give Japanese from other parts of the country the feeling that they might be in foreign country. At any rate it needs to be emphasized that although Westerners are prone to think of Japan and China as being sub-tropical, Sapporo, which was the site of the eleventh winter Olympics in 1972, enjoys a climate that is very similar to that of Scandinavia and New England.

The second point is the fact that Sapporo is a planned city and that the long march of Japan's history had no part to play in its evolution and construction. Such well-known Japanese cities as Tokyo, Osaka, and Nagoya all developed out of castle towns, while Sapporo was built in the middle of a plain with the idea that it would be a convenient point from which to conduct the defence of northern Japan and carry out the development of Hokkaido. In the language of the Ainu, the race that has lived in the northern parts of Japan since earliest recorded times, the name Sapporo means a dry, open area of land (or, according to another theory, a dried-up river) and when construction was commenced in 1869, there were just two Japanese households and a handful of Ainu households there. But this was the site for the construction of an artificial city measuring seven kilometres from north to south and six kilometres from east to west and intersected by wide ave-

Sapporo downtown

nues running across it at 120-metre intervals.

The Meiji government, having decided to introduce Western-style agriculture to Hokkaido, invited Horace Capron, who was then the United States Secretary of Agriculture, to inspect Hokkaido for himself and to give the government some advice on the development of Hokkaido, and offered him a salary that was higher than that received by any Japanese official at that time. Since the 1850's, Americans visiting Hokkaido had remarked that its climate was similar to that of New England and the person Capron invited to superintend agricultural education in Hokkaido was the President of Massachusetts College of Agriculture, W. E Clark. Clark was appointed head of Sapporo Agricultural College, which, as Hokkaido University, was later to become one of Japan's Imperial Universities, and he devoted his energy to education in American agricultural techniques. The notes taken by his students, which are preserved today in the library of Hokkaido University, are carefully written out in English. Clark knew nothing about Japanese agriculture, but he managed to educate a large number of intellectuals through the thorough education he offered his students in English rather than through its mainly agricultural content. It was in recognition of this that he became one of the best known Americans who have lived in Japan. Both Nitobe Inazo, who was later to be Secretary-General of the League of Nations, and Uchimura Kanzo, the Christian thinker, studied under Clark, but what they learnt from him seems to have been not so much agriculture as the New England Puritan spirit.

It cannot be said that the introduction of American agriculture was an unqualified success. But

American agriculture did make two important contributions to Sapporo's agricultural economy; beer and dairy products. Modern Sapporo is dominated by tertiary industry to the extent of 87.4 per cent and it is a consumer city, but the main products of its secondary industries are beer and such dairy products as butter and cheese, all of which were developed under the guidance of Americans. In spite of the belief that the cultivation of rice in Hokkaido was impossible, Japanese farmers persevered and their eventual success provided the foundation for the development of the whole of Hokkaido.

Before the Second World War, Sapporo was involved to some extent in the running of the Japanese colonial empire. It provided a model for new Japanese cities abroad, such as Toyohara in Sakhalin (now Yuzhno-Sakhalinsk) and Shinkyo in Manchuria (now Changchun).

Japanese civilization has produced two planned cities, one, Kyoto, in the early stages of its existence, and the other, Sapporo, in modern times. Neither Kyoto nor Sapporo, which respectively stand for the old and the new in Japanese cities, developed spontaneously. Both are rare examples of planned cities that have a grid pattern of intersecting roads at regular intervals. Kyoto was based on China, and Sapporo on the United States, and perhaps it can be said that they represent the starting point of Oriental civilization and the point to which occidental civilization has reached.

Every civilization is based on its own unalterable principles, and the Japanese civilization is based on flexibility. The growth of Sapporo is a sure sign of how healthy the Japanese civilization still is.

SONODA-Hidehiro

The Japanese colonies

Japan's modern history is a history of constant territorial expansion. The first new acquisition was Taiwan, which China handed over as a result of Japan's victory in the Sino-Japanese War in 1895. Japan's gains from the Russo-Japanese War of 1904-1905 comprised the southern half of Karafuto, or Sakhalin, and the Kwantung leased territory in China; Japan also gained Korea as a protectorate, and annexed it in 1910. Since Japan was on the victorious side in the First World War, she was able to take over the former German trusteeships in the South Sea islands. Thus within the space of just fifty years Japan almost doubled the size of its territory.

The initial impetus for Japan's programme of modernization in the Meiji period had come from the fear of becoming a colony of one of the Western powers, but in time a new aim emerged, that of catching up with the Western powers and becoming one of their equals. The token of a country of the first rank, seemed to be the possession of strong armed forces and a colonial empire. Taiwan and southern Karafuto were, in a sense, the prizes of war, but Korea's case was different. The annexation of Korea represented a clear determination to make a colony of it and this was the first step leading to Japan's subsequent career as a colonial power. The Russo-Japanese War had been fought under the pretext of the need to respect Korean sovereignty but as soon as Russia had been expelled from the region, Japan began to undermine Korean independence. In the nineteenth century there had been astonishingly little reflection on the whole notion of using military might to control other peoples in a colonial system, and Japan in the early twentieth century was no different, in this respect, from the Western powers.

The ideal colonial administration is probably one which minimizes the ability of the local population to resist the colonising power and facilitates the efficient use of the resources of the colony. Goto Shinpei based his ideal of colonial administration on the pattern of the British administration of India. After becoming the civil governor of Taiwan he did away with the system of colonial control based on force of arms and replaced it with a system that endeavoured to respect local customs, habits and practices as much as possible. Since accurate knowledge of the conditions in the colonies was one of the factors that determind whether colonial administration would be successful or not, university researchers and other specialists were invited to carry out the necessary research, and the results of their work were of great value for determining colonial administrative policy.

In 1906, Goto became the first president of the South Manchurian Railway Company, an enormous semi-official semi-private company which covered the leaseholds of Port Arthur (Lushun) and Dairen (Talien) and the railway and adjoining lands south of Changchun, all of which had been taken over from Russia after the Russo-Japanese War. The South Manchurian Railway Company was based on the model of the East India Company and Its operations covered an enormous range of activities, from communications, mining (the coal mines at Fushun), and heavy industry (the steel works at Anshan) to the settlement and exploitation of undeveloped areas and research of various kinds. Manchuria, under the Company, did not become a full-fledged colony until 1932, when the Japanese puppet government there declared the creation of the new state of Manchukuo. Nevertheless, a good deal of defacto colonisation was going on, for there were bans on the construction of railway facilities that might compete with those of the Company, and so on.

Goto was also involved in the formation of urban reconstruction plans for Taipei, Dairen, Mukden, Changchun and other cities. These reconstruction plans were conceived on a bold scale that would have been quite impossible in Japan itself. The experiences that were thus gained in the colonies were later put to use in Japan when Tokyo and Yokohama were destroyed in the Great Earthquake of 1923, for a reconstruction plan prepared by Goto and others was put into operation.

However, the impact of the colonies on Japan was not always so beneficial as this example might lead one to believe. There is a well-known phenomenon whereby events in the colonies which are beyond the tight control of the home government rebound on the home country and bring about political changes there.

The colonial administration on the Chinese mainland was at first based partly on the military might of the Kwantung army and partly on the administrative skills of the South Manchurian Railway Company, but in the course of time the Kwantung army became more and more interested in using its strength to try and bring about the actual colonisation of the whole of Manchuria. The involvement of the military in political matters had a particularly important role to play in the process leading up to the declaration of Manchukuo's 'independence', and the natural consequence of military involvement in civil matters there was the end of party politics in Japan itself and the large-scale involvement of the military in domestic Japanese politics. Japanese military leaders were prisoners of their ultranationalist ideologies and their political and intellectual convictions gradually turned Japan into a country with marked absolutist and xenophobic tendencies.

These political changes within Japan itself were reflected in administrative policy in the colonies too. The emphasis that had been placed up to this time on a rational and thoughtful model of colonial control faded away, and its place was taken by more irrational policies that sought to force Japanese culture on the colonised peoples. The Japanese language was made compulsory, as also were visits to Japanese Shinto shrines and the substitution of Japanese-type surnames for local surnames in 1937. They were also departures from the normal concept of colonial policy, given that the main point of having colonies was to squeeze them economically.

Nineteenth century colonialism had, for its aim, the acquisition of as much of the colonies' wealth as was possible. These aims were, however, gradually pushed into background by more rational considerations. But Japan, which in the twentieth century was desperately trying to become the last colonial power, did not succeed in developing a mature colonial policy of this kind. Just as its overly-rapid growth into a militaristic country ended up in failure, so too did its attempt to run a colonial system.

SONODA-Hidehiro

The Imperial Army and Navy

The conduct of war and the maintenance of standing armies were two of the major traditions Japan learnt from Europe in the nineteenth century. When Commodore Perry's fleet reached Japan in 1853, Japan had no standing national navy. And the groups of samurai who were the closest Japan had to an army were like mediaeval European knights, still armed with swords and spears. Firearms had of course already been introduced to Japan as early as the sixteenth century and were the most powerful weapons available in Japan, but even as late as the nineteenth century it was swords and spears that were regarded as the weapons appropriate to a samurai rather than guns and cannons.

There is nothing that is so easily and so obviously compared as levels of military development. It was abundantly clear to everybody that Japan was far behind in terms of its military power in the 1850's. Through the Opium War of 1840 Japan learnt for the first time of the military power and the philosophy of strength of the European civilization. China had only had weak forces at her disposal and it was thought that Japan would soon share her fate. So everyone in Japan was convinced that the building up of a strong army was essential if Japan's independence was to be preserved. Thus, from 1868 onwards, Japan devoted much of its energy to the creation of a powerful army and navy. Even during times of peace, enormous amounts of money were devoted to military expenditure, amounting sometimes to almost fifty per cent of the national budget.

In 1870, it was decided to model Japan's navy on that of England, and her army on that of France (later Germany), and naval and military academies were founded to give army and navy officers a Western-style training. The education provided in these academies was at first conducted in English, French and German, and naval officers were trained with the English gentlemen as their ideal, while the training of army officers looked to the Prussian army for its model. For this reason it is said that naval officers were inclined to be liberal in outlook, while army officers were closer to the authoritarian Prussian officer.

The social status of the military man was generally high. Officer education was conducted at the expense of the state and the method of recruitment involved an open competition, just as did the bureaucracy, so the most ambitious and the most able men could be recruited. One of the special features of the Imperial Army and Navy was that there was virtually none of the close relationships found in Europe between the officer corps and the aristocracy or financially privileged classes. It is true that at first most officers came from the former samurai class, not because of any social discrimination, but rather because there was no other class which considered soldiering to be its vocation. In 1873, a conscription system was introduced and by the end of the Second World War, when the army had a strength of some five and a half million, however authoritarian it may have been, it was not an aristocratic army like the German army used to be but rather an army of commoners: the same was true of the navy. An Englishman who taught at the Japanese naval academy before the war noted that the new officer recruits came from every class of Japanese society and that this had made a deep impression on him, in view of the very different situation in England.

Armed forces are generally large bureaucratic organizations. The Meiji Constitution of 1889 placed the emperor at the head of the armed forces of Japan as Commander-in-Chief, and it was the emperor rather than the government who was responsible for exercising supreme command over the army and navy. But since the emperors traditionally had made no decisions on their own initiative, this arrangement actually meant that the armed forces were free to decide on any armed action they pleased. The only control the government could exercise was indirect, via the annual military budget. This dual system of control by the government and the emperor (in fact, of course, the General Staff Office and the Naval General Staff Office) was liable to collapse in an instant if the armed forces failed to restrain themselves and refused to submit to indirect government control.

The fatal flaws in the system were brought out into the open over the signing of the London Naval Treaty of 1930. The treaty determined that the ratio of capital ships and aircraft carriers held by England, the United States and Japan would be 5 - 5 - 3. Since the First World War, the navy had looked upon the United States as Japan's potential enemy; it was therefore dissatisfied with the treaty and accused the government of usurping the right of supreme command. The following year, 1931, the Prime Minister was assassinated, and the armed forces began to involve themselves in political matters in earnest. The spirit of the Imperial Instructions to Soldiers and Sailors, which stated that they should have nothing to do with politics, was now reinterpreted, and the view adopted that political matters relating to military affairs came under the jurisdiction of the supreme commander rather than of the government. This put an end to the exercise of self-restraint by the armed forces.

The army and navy were vast organizations with a monopoly on physical violence. There was no force in Japan that could offer any resistance. The greatest failure of modern Japan was probably the failure to tame either politically or philosophically that demon, the armed forces, acquired from European civilization. Clausewitz had put forward the view that war was an instrument of politics, but in Japan politics had become a means of war. The army viewed the Soviet Union as the potential enemy of Japan, while the navy's potential enemy was the United States, and these views began to have an existence and reality of their own, such that they led to military exploits that took no account of Japan's real power. What is necessary for successful military adventures is a cool head and an aptitude for cold analysis. But for the Japanese the armed forces were too powerful a poison. They lacked the historical experience that might have enabled them to bring the armed forces to heel, and they were too naive. Thus, Japan failed in its adoption of an element of Western civilization.

SONODA-Hidehiro

The Provinces

The relationship between the provinces and the administrative and cultural centres of Japan is a very complex one. It is quite different from that in the United States, where diffusion and decentralization are the main characteristics, and different again from France, which is more centralized and where most activities are concentrated in Paris. Japan, in contrast with both the United States and France, enjoys both political centralization and cultural and social pluralism and diversity, and the two complement each other.

From region to region, there are astonishing differences in the various forms that social structure and cultural life take in the Japanese provinces. The main reason for this variety probably lies in the geography of the country, for the mountainous terrain that covers much of Japan has made a certain amount of regional independence inevitable. Thus until the introduction of a national education system in the Meiji period and later of national radio networks, there were considerable communication difficulties simply because the dialects that had developed in some regions were unintelligible to people from other regions. There were also differences, for example, in the social structure of the village: in western Japan there tended to be a fairly loose structure with the inhabitants participating on a more or less equal basis, but in eastern Japan there was a much more hierarchical arrangement.

The cultural and social variety described here became even more firmly established during Japan's feudal centuries. The entire country was divided up during the Edo period into units of territory parcelled out to nearly three hundred feudal barons, or daimyo. The domain of each daimyo was not only a unit of political administration but also a cultural unit, with its own customs, festivals and intellectual traditions. The largest daimyo domains, which were mostly to be found in western Japan, became cultural centres of some importance within the whole conspectus of Japanese culture. In some cases they developed to the point that they were miniature states with their own diplomacy, internal politics and government, and industrial policy. Cities such as Sendai, Kanazawa, Nagoya, Okayama, Hiroshima, Fukuoka, Kumamoto, and most of the other prefectural capitals in modern Japan, were cultural and political centres of importance during the Edo period and their significance remains the same today.

On the other hand, decentralization and regional self-government have not been much of a part of Japan's political culture, and this needs to be remembered. This was true even during the Edo period, when the daimyo received large tracts of land to administer and control. For, whereas the feudal barons in Western feudal systems enjoyed independence from the sovereign authority of the monarch, Japan in the Edo period was under a feudal system that came close to being absolutist. The daimyo had the rights to administer their territory, levy taxes and dispense justice, but their rights to maintain arms were subject to very strict controls. In the early part of the Edo period, it even happened, and quite often too, that daimyo would be removed from office or transferred to other domains. From this it should be clear that the position of the daimyo vis-à-vis the bakufu was weak and subservient.

Former Tsuruoka Police Station,
present Yamagata Prefectural Tsuruoka Chido Museum

The Meiji government, which came into existence after the fall of the Tokugawa bakufu, set about creating a still more centralized system of government. In 1871 the domains, which had been the focus of local feudal power, were abolished, and at the same time their military forces were disbanded and the territorial rights of the daimyo were taken over by the central government. In place of the domains, prefectures were established as the local administrative units of the central government, and governors were appointed by the central government to supervise the affairs of the prefectures. The administration of the armed forces, justice, the police, and even the prefectures themselves were now directly conducted by the central government, and the provinces were now even more subordinate to Tokyo, the administrative centre of the nation. Provincial government existed, of course, but it was not government conducted by the provinces.

In time, the prefectures came to acquire their own prefectural assemblies, and a system of municipal and rural administrative bodies was established, but these did not constitute local self-government so much as a means of seeing that the policies of the central government reached every corner of the nation.

It was because the provinces had their own traditions of political and cultural independence that the need was felt to create a system of centralized government in Japan. Loyalty to the region and particular attitudes, which had developed in each of the feudal domains, did not die away so quickly, however, and they survived in non-political forms, such as local educational associations, or they produced politicians who had made their way through local political organizations to the National Diet, where they represented local interests. Even today the desire to make one's way to one of the central cities, carve out a living for oneself there, and satisfy one's local pride by gaining recognition in a big city is still drawing many people from the towns and villages of Japan. For the Japanese, the central cities are gatherings of provincials from all parts of Japan, and in that sense Tokyo is just Japan's largest village. The urban energy and cultural diversity of the central cities are a reflection of the diversity and vitality of the provinces, and an illustration of the complex relationship between cities such as Tokyo and the provinces.

SONODA-Hidehiro

Modern Bureaucracy

The most powerful group in pre-war Japanese society was the bureaucracy. After the fall of the samurai as a class, it was the bureaucracy that took over the control and administration of Japan, but high positions in the bureaucracy were not gained through social rank, family connections or wealth. The bureaucracy was based instead on meritocratic principles, with recruitment conducted through open competition and subsequent advancement determined by individual achievement. A similar system in Europe would be the recruitment of the higher bureaucracy in France from the graduates of the École Polytechnique.

In the early Meiji period, the bureaucracy came for the most part from the ranks of the samurai class, who had both the drive to devote themselves to the administration of the state and the educational background needed. During the 1880's men of samurai background comprised about seventy-five per cent of the graduates of the Law Faculty of the Imperial University (now Tokyo University), which then as now was the principal recruiting ground for the bureaucracy. Before long, however, a system of uniform and universal compulsory education was introduced throughout Japan and this gradually reduced the gaps between the social classes. It then became more usual for commoners to be graduating from the university and becoming in turn successful candidates for the bureaucracy.

During the 1890's almost fifty per cent of those who passed the examinations for admission to the higher levels of the bureaucracy were of samurai origins, but the proportion had sunk to nearly twenty per cent by the end of the second decade of the twentieth century. Since the former samurai class only comprised some six per cent of the total population of Japan, even a figure of twenty per cent can be described as over-representation. But this was not a result of social discrimination; rather, it was the product of such factors as cultural motivation and levels of educational attainment. There was a great difference here from the situation in England, where alongside a system of open examinations for entrance to the administrative grades of the civil service, discrimination continued to be exercised under the guise of an interview system.

The bureaucracy achieved its unrivalled power in Japan not simply as a result of the centralization of powers in the modern Japanese state. As successful candidates who had passed open examinations designed to test their academic aptitude, they were in a sense an embodiment of the new meritocratic ideals, and this was an important factor, too. In contrast to Great Britain and Germany, there were very few members of the aristocracy to be found in Japan's bureaucracy, and this is a point worth noting. In Europe the recruitment of the bureaucracy and the military may well have been based on meritocratic principles, but the European education system was anything but meritocratic and embodied a considerable amount of social segregation. This led to a state of affairs in which large numbers of administrative and military professionals were of aristocratic origins. In Japan, by contrast, since everybody received the same kind of education and since the competitive examinations were conducted on a fair and impartial basis, it was no easy matter for members of the aristocracy to pass the examinations and thereby gain entrance to the bureaucracy. It was for these reasons that the Japanese bureaucracy, which was drawn from all classes of society, was able to establish itself as a powerful body. The social prestige of the bureaucracy was high, too, and in court the bureau chief of a government ministry had precedence over viscounts and barons, and the Chief of the General Staff had precedence over dukes.

The central bureaucratic administration before the Second World War consisted of the Finance, Foreign Affairs, Justice, Education, Agriculture and Commerce, Posts, Railways, War and Navy Ministries and the Home Ministry, which exercised a supervisory role over the population via the police and local government. Bureaucrats who had passed the Higher Civil Service Examination were given accelerated promotion after being assigned to one or other of these ministries and their careers differed from those of the ordinary bureaucrats. They exercised their considerable powers with a sense of mission, a sense of belonging to an elite and pride at being involved in the running of the country.

In Japan the Diet and the political parties have to be taken into consideration, too, in connection with the role of the bureaucracy. The existence of the party cabinet system, which only became established in the twentieth century, may suggest that the senior bureaucrats exist only to serve politicians faithfully. But from 1900-1945, twenty seven of thirty Prime Ministers came from the bureaucracy.

The large number of ex-bureaucrats who became Prime Ministers can be explained by the eagerness of the political parties to adopt leading members of the bureaucracy as party leaders in the hope of extending their influence and power. Between the bureaucrats on the one hand and the industrialists, landowners and journalists who constituted the bulk of the ordinary party politicians on the other, there were, of course, differences in ways of thinking and acting, but when it came to assuming responsibility for the governance of the country cabinet, there was plenty of room for a compromise to be worked out. The pre-war constitution, which was enacted in 1889, contains no clear mention of the party cabinet system; under its provisions, the Prime Minister was selected by a group of so-called Elder Statesmen, or Genro, and then confirmed in his appointment by the Emperor. And it was members of the bureaucracy rather than party politicians who enjoyed the confidence of the Genro when it came to selecting a Prime Minister. Therefore the majority parties in the Diet were eager to have at their head a powerful member of the bureaucracy, and it was in this way that members of the bureaucracy came to play an important role outside the bureaucracy itself.

These political traditions continued after the war, too: the parties could not afford to ignore the talent and policy-planning abilities many bureaucrats had, and so post-war cabinets have similarly been filled with former bureaucrats, including the post of Prime Minister. The generally poor quality of party politicians has been an important factor here, too, but the Japanese people waver between opposition to bureaucratic types of organisation and trust in the excellence of the bureaucracy itself.

SONODA-Hidehiro

Posts and Telecommunications

Japan is a small island country lying off the eastern coast of the vast expanse of continental China. One does not have to be Japanese in order to know this elementry fact of geography, but it does bear looking into. There is no denying that, in terms of total land area, Japan is one of the smaller nations; however, when it comes to length, this chain of islands rivals the eastern seabord of the United States of America. And Tokyo, the capital city, is situated roughly in the centre of the chain, meaning that a considerable distance lies between it and either extremity.

History tells us that, as part of the process by which a nation evolves, the feudal system of the medieval period collapses and a powerful central government is established in its place. However, a necessary condition for this evolution is the provision of a communication network which will enable the swift and secure transmission of political directives between the seat of government and the provinces. For this reason, the geographical distance between the capital and the various provinces is especially significant: For instance, London to Edinburgh is approximately 450 kilometres, Paris to Marseilles 700 kilometres, Berlin to Frankfurt 500 kilometres, and Rome to Genoa 500 kilometres. In contrast, the distance between Tokyo and Kagoshima — a city in southern Kyushu which in 1877 was the site of the last organized military revolt against the central government — is about 1000 kilometres. Until the Meiji Restoration of 1868, the country had been divided into numerous domains, each under the direct control of a daimyo, or feudal lord. Although answerable to the bakufu government, the daimyo enjoyed considerable independence; maintaining their own private armies, they were in a state of permanent rivalry. Thus, for Japan, the creation of a nationwide communications network was a matter of immediate political significance.

With the Meiji Restoration, a centralized government was established and, in the following year, a telegraphic system was introduced linking Tokyo with nearby Yokohama. Two years later, in 1871, the service was extended as far as Nagasaki on the far western coast of Japan proper (comprising the four main islands: Honshu, Shikoku, Kyushu and Hokkaido). In 1874 there was an armed uprising in Saga, not far from Nagasaki, and the new telegraph was to play an important part in its suppression; this early example of war reportage was published under the title of *"The Saga Telegraphic Chronicle"* by the popular novelist Kanagaki Robun (1829 – 1894). By the end of the decade, the telegraph wires had spread over the entire country, linking all the major cities. The growth of the telegraph and telephone networks was thus extraordinarily fast; together with the developing railroad system, these played a decisive role in the political unification of Japan.

The successful modernization of a country needs of a political structure that is both powerful and stable and this needs, in turn, a comprehensive communication system, that includes networks for transportation. Speed is of the essence, a point that is illustrated by a comparison with the situation in China.

In the early twentieth century in China there still

existed various military cliques in the provinces which were independent of the authority of the central government. One reason for this state of affairs was undoubtedly the enormous size of the country, but it would seem that the failure to establish a system for the swift transmission of political directives was an important contributing factor. In 1906, the time required for the transmission of the administration's orders to the provinces was as follows: Zhili (the region surrounding Beijing), 4 days; Fengtian, 7 days; Hunan, 15 days; Sichuan, 50 days; Xinjiang, 90 days; and Xizang (Tibet), 165 days. In Japan, according to a regulation formulated in 1883, government proclamations and edicts were to be delivered to the suburbs of Tokyo on the same day, to Kyoto and Osaka in 4 days, Aomori in 10 days, and Kagoshima in 12 days. But the difference between the Chinese and Japanese systems was not only one of speed. Later a railway system centred on the capital was built up and, by the turn of the century, Japan was able to boast nationwide railroad, telegraph and telephone networks that rivalled those of Europe and America. China, meanwhile, had only railways of the decentralized type, built to link agricultual centres to their nearest seaports for the transportation and export of produce. This is a typical colonial pattern of development.

The real difference between the communication system developed in Japan and those of the West lies in the road network. It is often pointed out that the horse-drawn carriage and cart was never a common form of transport in Japan; During the Edo period (1600 – 1867), cargo transportation relied on waterways. What overland transport there was took place on the backs of pack-horses; The use of carts was severely restricted for the reason that it conflicted with the interests of those who owned the ships and pack-horses. For instance, in Osaka — the passage of carts over the many bridges in the city was banned, and later the use of carts during the night was also outlawed. In fact it was not until 1862 that carts could at last move freely along major highways for the transport of goods. Then in 1866 the use of horse-drawn carriages was allowed, but only after resident Westerners had imported them for their own transport. It was in the Meiji period (1868 – 1912) that a long-distance carriage service was established, but it failed to prosper thanks to the competition offered by the railways which were already being laid. For this reason, Japan's roads were never really more than footpaths, a situation that did not change until the postwar motorization of the country. Even now, despite the fact that Japan is the largest producer of automobiles in the world, road construction has not yet caught up. Although both modern forms of transport, the train and the car are poles apart: the former, orderly and punctual, running smartly along its gleaming tracks; is largely controlled by government agencies; the latter by the whim of the individual.

SONODA-Hidehiro

1 Japan's Two Constitutions

In modern times Japan has had two quite different constitutions. The first of these was the Imperial Japanese Constitution promulgated in 1889, and the second was the Constitution of Japan promulgated in 1947. The former was based on the Prussian Constitution and on the principle of imperial sovereignty, while the latter was created by the General Headquarters of the United States Army of Occupation under the direction of General McArthur, the Supreme Commander of the

Celebration for the promulgation of the Japanese Constitution in 1946

(by favour of Kyodo)

Allied Powers, and was based on the principle of popular sovereignty. There can be no doubt that the new constitution was forced on Japan by the Occupation Forces. Some Japanese conservatives argue that since the new constitution was forced upon Japan in this way, it does not belong to Japan and should be revised, but of course it is equally true that the Meiji Constitution of 1889 did not belong to Japan either under such an interpretation, given that it was modelled on that of Prussia.

The Meiji Constitution was the first constitution to be formally promulgated in Asia, and this is something the Japanese have tended to be proud of. However, the principles on which it was based and its fundamental theoretical framework were the products of European society and not of Japanese society, and so there was constantly a discrepancy between what was actually prescribed in the constitution and the practice of constitutional government. Another way of putting it would be to say that there had never yet been in Japan any attempt to rationalize political practice and to codify it in the form of a constitution. Take for example the notion of a constitutional monarch: In Europe the monarch was understood to be desirous of using his discretionary powers to the maximum and it was held to be the task of the national assembly to keep the monarch in check. Pre-war Japan has to be described as a constitutional monarchy, for there was a hereditary monarch in the form of the emperor and a constitution in existence that provided the political basis of the state. However, the emperor system in Japan differed from the constitutional monarchies of Europe, and instead of being a person who exercised political authority the monarch was in Japan a symbol of the state. In the post-war constitution the emperor is described as a symbol of national unity and in this respect the position he enjoys now differs little in fact from that which he enjoyed under the Meiji Constitution.

There can be no doubt that under the Meiji Constitution the Emperor enjoyed considerable powers including the rights of supreme command of the armed forces, of the conduct of foreign relations and of the issuing of imperial rescripts. But it was only because the constitution had been modelled on constitutional ideas developed by the European nations that these rights were mentioned in the Meiji Constitution at all, and the reality in Japan was quite different. Insofar as political matters were concerned, the ideal for the emperor was held to be the lack of any political will whatsoever, and it fact there were very few matters on which he alone had to decide. The situation that the Emperor found himself in was one that would have been incomprehensible in European terms and was one that not only applied to the Emperor but had also applied to many of Japan's feudal leaders in the past.

For the Japanese the constitution is a matter of form or principle, and as such it is not a reality, even though it may exert some control over reality and influence the course of events. It is only by ignoring this fact and trying to make a reality of the constitution that such bodies as the Movement for the Clarification of the National Policy could have come into existence. This movement believed that the Emperor was the sovereign of Japan and as such that he should enjoy absolute power and it criticised the view popularized by constitutional scholars that the Emperor was one of the organs of state, a view that placed emphasis on the Emperor's role rather than on his supposed power. The Movement for the Clarification of the National Policy sought, in other words, to put the constitutional principle into reality.

The New Constitution is widely accepted by Japanese as an expression of values to be followed in principle. The pacifism and fundamental human rights embodied in it are approved by most Japanese, irrespective of the way in which it was formulated and promulgated. This is largely due to the contrast with the Japanese pre-war experience - the launching of a war of aggression, the severe curtailment of freedom of expression, and the suppression of fundamental human rights. The possibility of unnecessary confusion will only arise if it is forgotten that principle and reality are two different things and if, for example, irresponsible pacifism or notions of human rights that ignore Japanese social customs gain currency. The ideas expressed in the constituion are principles and they are principles that should be respected, but even if they are to be translated into reality it is essential that an element of real understanding be used.

SONODA-Hidehiro

The Family System

Modern Japan has experienced two completely different types of family law, a law which defines the rights and responsibilities of the members of a family. The first of these was established in 1898, while the second was enacted at the behest of the Occupation Forces in the postwar period and is the one currently in force. The latter is founded on the negation of the patriarchal household system which had formed the crux of the former legislation. The family, of all social systems, is perhaps the most resistant to any outside artificial pressure designed to force a change. Nevertheless, two diametrically opposed codes of family law have been enacted in Japan during the last century. How is it possible for such a situation to have come about?

The code of 1898 was, in fact, compiled and promulgated eight years previously. It was designed to annul and replace the Family Law (legal scholars use the more correct term "kinship law") which was to have come into force in 1893. This latter code, consigned to oblivion before it reached the statute books, was the cause of a famous controversy - known as the "Civil Code Dispute" - a landmark in the history of Japanese thought. The ill-fated code which was replaced had been modelled on the Civil Code of France, a code of law founded on the principle of consanguinity and featuring an individualist interpretation of the nature of the family which seriously contradicted the concept of the family held by the Japanese people at that time. To take one example: according to the French system, a man's wife has no legal kinship with his parents, whereas in

Japan it was customarily considered that a wife, on the occasion of her marriage, became a member of her husband's household and from that day was in effect a new daughter to her husband's parents. In those days, as indeed today, it was a very widespread custom for the young couple to live under the same roof as the husband's parents. For this reason, it was feared that the French-style individualist interpretation of the family would serve to destroy the patrilocal morality that bound the Japanese family. The reactionaries protested that "The Civil Code will destroy filial piety!" Filial piety is, of course, the central concept of Confucian morality, a code of conduct imported from China that emphasizes the respect due to a parent from the child. However, this period was witnessing the development of patriarchalism (the identification of the state as one large family) in Japan, and consequently people began to think of relations within the state as they did relations within the family. From this point of view, there was basically no difference between the filial piety demanded by the head of the family, and the loyalty demanded by the head of state, the emperor. Therefore, to the reactionaries the problem was not limited to the family alone; they believed that the destruction of Confucian morality which would be caused by the proposed Code would surely pose a danger to the survival of the state as well as that of the family.

In France, relations within the family depended on the individual, an independent unit; the whole was merely the sum of the parts, in other words. In Japan, however, the traditional concept of the family was that of a 'system', an indivisible entity. First we have a community of people bound by blood ties and living together as a 'family'; individuals then acquire membership in this community by means of either marriage or birth. What was considered important in Japan was not the continuation of the blood line, but the continued existence of the 'family' itself. In Europe, if the last member of an aristocratic family were to die leaving no heirs, the estate would be confiscated by the sovereign. In Japan, though, such a fate could be avoided and the property retained by means of appointing a fictitious heir, adopting a 'son' into the family: what received precedence was the continuation of the family rather than the lineage.

The primary concern and responsibility of the head of a Japanese family was this continuity; the organic community around him was a charge, passed down from his ancestors, which by whatever means must be handed on to his successor. The prewar Civil Law granted the head of the family considerable power to decide on matters affecting its members, such as those involving living quarters or marriages. This is a type of patriarchal system. The family head could be described as a caretaker autocrat with responsibility for the household and, above all, for the continued existence of the family and its place in the flow of history. The other members might have had to bend to the patriarch's will, but for them the family was the final bastion that protected their economic livelihood. And it was because of this security provided by the family that, when the new postwar code replaced primogeniture with a formula by which the estate was divided up among the heirs, traditional family life remained virtually unchanged.

The prewar Civil Law was actually based on the strict ethics of the samurai household and thus overemphasized the authority of the paterfamilias, according him more power than was customarily found in the average Japanese family. In sharp contrast to this, the civil rights introduced after the war were modelled on the western political concept of democracy and abolished the prewar family system. But the individualistic urge was not very strong among the Japanese; so, although the law may have changed considerably, the reality of family life was much the same. A conservative ideologue has described the Japanese family as the bedrock of the imperialistic state, while a progressive social commentator has stated that the Japanese people really hated the traditional family system. Both observations may contain some truth, but neither are completely right.

Even if the Japanese family has not changed much so far, however, it may do so in the future. As an organization designed for the communal protection of its members' livelihoods, the *raison d'être* of the traditional family requires a harsh economic climate. It also demands the respect for harmony within the group in order to stay together. The rapid economic growth and accompanying prosperity of the postwar period, however, together with the steady infiltration of individualistic notions, have already succeeded in destroying the two conditions necessary for the survival of the traditional family system.

SONODA-Hidehiro

Peace and War in Japan

The nineteenth century is sometimes said to have been an age of peace, and it is indeed true that not very many serious wars broke out between the conclusion of the Napoleonic wars and the outbreak of the First World War in 1914. But for Japan, by contrast, it was in fact the nineteenth century that marked the onset of a period in which she fought a number of wars. First there was the war between Great Britain and the province of Satsuma in Kyushu in 1863, followed the next year by the Shimonoseki War and the First Bakufu-Choshu War; then in 1866 there was the Second Bakufu-Choshu War, and in 1868 a series of battles that took place in eastern Japan and that are collectively known as the Boshin War. Next, in 1877, there was Japan's last civil war, the South-West War or, as it is known in English, the Satsuma Rebellion. In 1894 and 1904 Japan engaged China and then Russia in war, and thus the scale of Japan's wars was constantly on the increase.

Since Japan had enjoyed more than two hundred years of peace after the suppression of the Shimabara Rebellion of 1638, she found herself at the end of the Edo period with little knowledge or understanding of war and little familiarity with the modern technology of warfare. She had to learn both of these from the countries of Europe. According to a book by Takagi Sokichi, the number of wars fought by a number of major countries during the 460 years between 1480 and 1941 was as follows: England, seventy-eight; France, seventy-one; Spain, sixty-four; Russia, sixty-one; Austria, fifty-two; Italy, twenty-five; Germany, twenty-three; the United States, thirteen; and Japan, nine. These figures give a clear idea of how closely the development of European civilization was tied to the practice of war.

After the arrival of Commodore Perry's fleet and the opening-up of Japan in the 1850s, Japan became a convert to the modern idea of war. It acquired the philosophy and technology of war and these gradually changed the nature of the country. In 1875 Japan took the same measures in respect of Korea that she herself had experienced at the hands of the United States in the person of Commodore Perry. In other words, she used force of arms to intimidate Korea into bringing its period of national isolation to an end. The build-up of Japanese military strength had initially been designed to protect Japan's independence from the powers of western Europe, but the Korean expedition was indicative not simply of a passive posture of defence but rather of the ambition to move out and seek concessions from other countries. Japan's move into Korea hurt the pride and damaged the interests of China, for China had long been the country to exercise control over Korea. The result of this conflict of interests was the Sino-Japanese War of 1894-95.

Japan's victory in that war spelt the end of the traditional international order in the Far East. It also turned Japan's feelings of inferiority towards China as the centre of civilization into a feeling of superiority. It was regarded as inevitable that Japan would advance into the Chinese mainland, and the military strength that had been built up for the purposes of defence began to take on the appearance more and more of aggressive might. The rights and concessions of the European powers in China awaited the onslaught of the

Japanese army.

The Russo-Japanese War was the most successful of all the wars Japan had ever experienced. Japan, after all, fought on equal terms with Russia, formerly one of the strongest military power in the world, and in the Battle of Tsushima inflicted a historic, crushing defeat on the Russian Baltic Fleet, which had sailed all the way from Europe. In Japan, the advance of Russia into the Far East had been viewed as a grave threat to the nation, but at the time Japan had little confidence in her ability to win a war with Russia, and no funds with which to conduct such a war. It was foreign funds which provided the necessary finance. A war of this kind, people at the time considered, could hardly be a war of aggression - it was a defensive war and their cause was surely just.

After Japan had secured victory in the Russo-Japanese War, she moved further and further in the direction of becoming a fully-fledged imperialist nation. She extended her rights and concessions on the Chinese mainland, took possession of the positions regarded as essential for the defence of the home islands, and in 1932 went so far as to set up a puppet state in Manchuria which was subservient to Japan's wishes. Japan had joined the imperialist club later than the other members and now she was pressing ahead with a hasty and ill-considered programme of expansion. When Japan launched total war against China in 1937 without any declaration of war, the conduct of events was so haphazard and unplanned that it is difficult to call it an invasion. The extension of one battle-front led to the extension of another, and by 1941 the Japanese army found itself in French Indo-China. This proved to be the decisive point of confrontation with the United States, which had already for some time been trying to call a halt to Japanese military operations in China. With the cooperation of England and the Netherlands, the United States launched an oil embargo on Japan and demanded the total withdrawal of Japanese troops from China.

The possibilities open to Japan at this juncture were two: either to undertake a fundamental revision of existing policy towards China, or to gamble on a military adventure. At the time Japan's production of essential commodities such as oil, iron, pig iron, copper and aluminium was one seventy-eighth that of the United States. No calculating aggressor would surely have launched a military adventure against so relatively well-supplied a power as the United States. But Japan's rights and concessions on the Chinese mainland had been bought with the blood of many Japanese and it was impossible for sentimental soldiers to think of giving them up altogether. And they could not but feel that since the United States, England and the Netherlands had also been engaging in colonization, there was no reason why Japan should not do likewise. They certainly felt that it was unreasonable and illogical for Japan alone to be criticised for doing what everybody else was doing: Japan's military activities were fundamentally the same as those practised by the countries of the West. If Japan was acting wrongfully, then so too were the countries that were criticising her. But what is certainly true is that Japan was not as successful an imperialist nation as the Western countries that had shown her the way.

SONODA-Hidehiro

Industrial Revolution

Japan's industrial revolution began in the last decade of the nineteenth century, continuing up until the end of the Russo-Japanese War (1904-1905), although its effects were felt for long after. Spinning was to take pride of places among Japan's light industries. For instance, from 1890 to 1900 the number of spindles in use increased three times, while output grew four times, and Japan became an exporter. In 1890 the population of the country had been less than forty million, but by 1912 it had climbed to over fifty million. Meanwhile, during the same period the agricultural population shrank to almost half of its previous size.

Despite these revolutionary changes to Japan and her industries, this period has never really been thought of as an "industrial revolution" as such. The reason for this is that a better understanding of the situation is obtainable by means of a political interpretation of events. Thirty years prior to Japan's industrial revolution the country had been subject to a political revolution - referred to as the Meiji Restoration - of far greater historical significance. The industrial revolution can be seen as having taken place on the initiative of the new Meiji government, and as having been the fruit of its policy to strengthen the state both economically and militarily. In this regard, Japan was somewhat different from Britain, if we make a comparison with the country in which the original Industrial Revolution took place where it occurred naturally and spontaneously, and has immense historical importance as the source of various social changes, as well as reforms of the political system.

In Japan, on the other hand, the chain of cause and effect led not from economy to society to politics, but was entirely the reverse. Directly as a result of a political initiative, a number of policies - such as the political unification of the country, the abolition of the pre-modern social stratification and the creation of a modern army - were put into effect; the modernization of industry was one of these. Needless to say, the reason why these policies could be put into practice was that there already existed the necessary foundation - educational, social and technical - which had been gradually developing among the populace since the Edo period (1600 - 1867). Another important factor was that such countries as Britain, France, Germany and the United States of America had already achieved industrial revolution, thus furnishing Japan with more than one model. Japan was thus in a position to make use of technology transfer to greatly speed up the difficult process of industrialization. Beginning in the 1870's, the Meiji government set up spinning mills and other enterprises, under both governmental and prefectural management, in order to foster the development of modern industry. The factories themselves, however, were designed not so much as profitable businesses but as training centres for technicians; the technology was imported directly from the advanced countries of the West and their finances were permanently in the red. The expensive equipment included so-called "mule" spinning machines from Britain, and reeling machines from France. Eventually these mills were sold off to the public; however, because they were mostly small enterprises hampered by unfavorable locations, the majority of them were destined to fail. However, because of the experience built up over this early period, the spinning industry in the private sector was able to gradually build up strength. By the time the Sino-Japanese War (1894 - 1895) had come to an end, Korea and China opened up as new markets for cotton goods, and the spinning industry responded by growing rapidly.

The development of Japan's heavy industry was in greater measure due to the guiding role played by government factories. First, the navy began building warships at shipyards directly under its control, and at major naval ports such as Yokosuka and Kure, it established facilities for the manufacture and repair of cannons and other weaponry. The army similarly set up its own ordnance factories. Representative of these government-controlled enterprises was Yahata Seitetsu, an ironworks which began operations in 1901. Built to produce steel for use in the manufacture of weapons and rails, in 1915 it turned out 247,000 tons of pig iron, 382,000 tons of steel ingots, and 265,000 tons of rolled steel; these figures represent over 70% of total production in Japan at that time.

As can be seen, Japan's industrial revolution came about as a direct consequence of the Meiji government's policies to promote new industries, expand production and strengthen the country both economically and militarily; for this reason it has never been accorded special interest or concern as an important historical phenomenon in its own right. Later, however, this Japanese style of industrial modernization came to be considered as a model for many developing nations, anxious to duplicate its success. It is true to say that Japan was the first country to systematically plan the modernization of its industry by means of government policies that looked to more developed countries for inspiration. Furthermore, it is only natural to imagine that, if one were to search out the reasons for Japan's success, one might be able to discover the "secret" of how to create an industrialized economy. But, can Japan really serve as a useful model for the developing countries? Unfortunately, the answer is no.

Japan's success had a lot to do with timing. In the latter half of the nineteenth century, the difference in industrial level between those western countries which had experienced industrial revolution and the developing countries of the time - including Japan - was relatively small. In comparison, the gap that now exists in the latter half of the twentieth century between the industrialized and developing nations is a great deal larger. Progress used to be slower. Japan began its industrial revolution a century behind Britain, but recent research has shown that steam engines were still not being used on a wide scale in British factories. In 1883, when Japan's first steam-powered spinning mill was established, it was equipped with electric lighting. At the time, Europe and America were entering the final stage of development, aiming at the completion of the industrialization process. One after another, new technologies were springing up, and those best positioned for introducing these and exploiting new opportunities were countries like Japan, unencumbered by old technologies. As a result of experiencing the last industrial revolution of the nineteenth century, Japan was thus able to become an industrialized state on a par with the advanced, industrialized countries of the West.

SONODA-Hidehiro

The Labour Movement

There are a surprising number of people in countries outside Japan who think that Japan's high productivity depends on the lack of proper trade unions. They have heard that robots have been introduced into the work-place in large numbers and that industrial workers work in an orderly fashion, and they appear to suppose that these things are only possible because the rights of the working men and women are not recognized in Japan. The fact is, however, that in Japan, labour rights are protected as much as the rights of European or American workers, if not more so, and there are furthermore strong labour unions.

Labour unions are essential for the protection of the rights of working men and women, but if they are too strong they stand in the way of the efficient management of industrial enterprises. Each country has to find its own way with these two considerations in mind and to work out some form of compromise between the unions on the one hand and the employers on the other.

Most labour unions in Japan espouse the principles of agreement and cooperation in their dealings with their employers, and they recognize the fact that employers and employees in the same enterprise share the same fate. Even the most militant Japanese unions at the end of the nineteenth century inserted into their statutes the hope that the companies their members worked for would prosper and the understanding that the union would in fact sink or swim with the company. The Friendly Societies, which formed the main current of the labour movement before the war, also aimed at cooperation between workers and management and hoped for friendliness at the workplace, mutual assistance, the cultivation of moral character and technological improvement as well as social improvement. These tendencies grew stronger as the pattern of life-long employment became the norm and as it became more usual for employees to spend many years working for the same company. The enterprise became a kind of cooperative body, and as fellow members all those employed by it shared its fate.

The social relationships between the employees and employers did not develop in this way as the result of any efforts on the unions' part to promote cooperation between capital and labour. Rather, they stem from the fact that most workers came from country districts and brought to the companies they worked for the sense of a stable moral order based on cooperation that they had been imbued with since childhood.

Japanese industrial relations were originally based on feudal relations with the later addition of a bureaucratic framework, so they retained to a considerable degree a social order based on status within the enterprise. In railway companies, for example, the engine drivers had to prostrate themselves before the station master's assistant when receiving their orders. It hardly needs to be added that the low status of the engine driver was reflected in the low wages he received. The position of workers in industrial enterprises therefore presented a great social problem. It is difficult to determine just how much the unions contributed to the improvement of wage differentials and the position of the workers within the enterprise, for less than ten per cent of enterprises were unionized before the war and the levelling out of wages and status differentials made progress irrespective of whether a given company was unionized or not.

The unions and the labour movement as a whole did however achieve positive results in such areas as the eight-hour day and the improvement of working conditions and in their demands for universal manhood suffrage. The House of Representatives, the lower house of the Japanese Diet, was at that time based on a limited franchise restricted to males who paid above a certain level of taxation, but the labour movement pressed for a universal suffrage in which levels of taxation would be irrelevant; the only possible way for the unions of having their demands accepted and put into practice since striking was all but illegal.

Union activity was however subject to repressive laws and these encouraged part of the labour movement and some intellectuals belonging to the socialist movement to take more extreme positions, and the emergence of greater numbers of extremists in its turn prompted still more repressive legislation from the government. In 1925 the demands for universal manhood suffrage finally met with success, but at the same time the draconian Peace Preservation Law was passed, which forbade the formation of groups seeking to change the national or political structure or denying the legitimacy of private property. The labour movement was emasculated as a political force by this legislation.

On the other hand the unions' demands for improvements in factory working conditions were gradually met as industrial enterprises came to take on more and more the character of cooperative bodies. The owners and managers of firms accepted these developments by taking the view that the enterprise constituted one big family in which all were members together, while they were accepted on the union side with the understanding that unions and management shared the same fate.

Industrial relations in Japan thus seem to be characterised by emphasis on cooperation rather than conflict, but could this be simply because of the weakness of Japanese labour unions? After all, enterprises are in fact associations and cannot become communities. Whatever the right answer to this question, it is at least clear that labour practices in Japan differ greatly from those in Western countries. And while in Japan the development of cooperative relations between management and employees has eliminated the wage and status differentials that used to exist between blue-collar and white-collar workers, the trade unions of Europe and North America, where the labour movement had its origins, have yet to achieve such success in this area. This is not a matter of one system being better than another. Rather, the cooperative nature of Japanese industrial enterprises is fundamentally different from the nature of European and North American enterprises, which more closely resemble associations of people with various skills. These differences have to be borne in mind when assessing the roles of labour unions in the two industrial systems.

SONODA-Hidehiro

1 Earthquakes

Do you know what the word tsunami means? Macmillan's Contemporary Dictionary defines it as a "swift, powerful ocean wave caused by an underwater earthquake and causing great destruction to any land area it strikes." In origin this word is Japanese. There are not many Japanese words that have found their way into the English language, but perhaps this example is not unexpected as many people think of Japan as being a country famous for its earthquakes.

From far-off Europe, Japan used to be seen as one of the exotic countries of the Far East. If such a land, shrouded in mystery, can offer not only a wonderful culture but also bizarre natural phenomena, the foreigner's interest is heightened all the more. In his book *Things Japanese*, the famous orientalist Basil Hall Chamberlain wrote thus:

> "Oh! how I wish I could feel an earthquake!" is generally among the first exclamations of the newly-landed European.

From this it can be seen that, in the late nineteenth century, Japan had already acquired a reputation for its earthquakes. Just to imagine that *terra firma*, that immovable presence beneath one's feet, might actually shake must have been very curious and very exciting to the Europeans of that age.

One of these visitors from Europe was a young British scholar, just twenty-five years old, called John Milne. He, however, had not come to experience Japan's famous earthquakes; in 1876 he was employed to lecture on mining and geology at the College of Engineering (later to become the Imperial University College of Engineering). He returned home in 1895, but during his nineteen years in Japan he experienced a life of "earthquakes at breakfast, earthquakes at lunch, earthquakes at supper, and earthquakes when asleep." In such an environment Milne, who was anyway curious by nature, came round to thinking that a person could not help becoming interested in the earthquake phenomenon. Milne's description of his experience in Japan is, needless to say, somewhat exaggerated; however, it is true to say that earthquakes were almost a common occurrence, especially in the Tokyo region in which he was living. It was as a result of this "moving" experience that Milne switched disciplines from mining to seismology, the study of earthquakes. In fact, in would be more accurate to say that Milne was responsible for founding this new branch of science, thus earning a place in history.

After returning to Britain, John Milne made use of his experiences and the knowledge he had gathered in Japan to promote the scientific study of earthquakes. As a result, seismology became a new branch of science in Europe.

Why is it that earthquakes are so common in Japan? According to the theory of plate-tectonics – the most generally accepted theory at present – the reason lies in the fact that the heavy Pacific plate is continually burrowing under its neighbour, the Asian plate which supports the continent. This action gives rise to massive friction and distortion, directly below the Japanese archipelago. These deformations gradually build up until the strain energy rises above a threshold level, at which point everything suddenly snaps back releasing terrific energy in the form of an earth-

quake. In other words, as long as the Japanese islands sit on the abrasive border of the Asian and
Pacific plates, the Japanese people will continue
their uneasy relationship with earthquakes.

The tsunami caused by earthquakes have always been a source of worry for the Japanese. In
the century or so since the beginning of the Meiji
period (1868 – 1912), Japan has experienced over
twenty large and extremely powerful earthquakes
with a magnitude of 7.0 or over. If one were to include all those quakes large enough to be felt,
then the number would rise to several hundred
times that. The first large earthquake experienced
by Japan since 1868 was one which occurred in
the Nōbi region in 1891; it registered a magnitude
of 7.9, and the aftershocks continued for another
ten years. Over seven thousand lives were lost
and 140,000 houses completely destroyed.
However, just five years later an earthquake in the
northern Sanriku region caused a huge tsunami,
towering as high as 24.4 metres, which claimed
the lives of 27,000 people.

Perhaps the most famous earthquake of modern Japan is the Great Kantō Earthquake of 1923.
With a magnitude of 7.9, at the top of the scale, it
struck mainly at Tokyo and Yokohama, the nerve
centres of the country. Because of the importance
of the region, it had very serious consequences
to the political, industrial, cultural and other
aspects of life. The resulting fires raged for three
days and nearly 100,000 people died. The downtown area of Tokyo, which had until then still preserved much of old Edo (the name by which the
city was known prior to 1868), was reduced to
ashes, thus severing a link with the past.

The horror which one feels during an earthquake derives from a sense of betrayal: suddenly

one can no longer trust the ground under one's feet, the *terra firma* which is the basis of all that is sure in this world. If the earth shakes, man loses faith in everything about him and is liable to fall into a state of panic. In an attempt to deal with earthquakes, the Japanese have developed quake-resistant buildings and also made an extensive study of possible methods of forecasting future shocks. Unfortunately, despite these efforts, the Japanese are still forced to live under the ever-present threat of a major earthquake. The beautiful islands that make up Japan boast a mild climate and some spectacular scenery, but they are perched on a very unreliable foundation. This is something which may well have had a part in shaping the mentality of the people themselves. Whatever the truth, there is no escaping the fact that the Japanese are fated to live in a beautiful garden in which they can never really sleep in carefree peace.

SONODA-Hidehiro

Fissured road (Yomiuri Newspaper)

Hiroshima and the Atomic Bomb

On 6 August 1945, a B-29 bomber of the United States Air Force dropped a single bomb on Japan. It was three metres long and seventy-one centimetres in diametre, and it weighed four tons, but its nickname was 'Little Boy'. It was the first atomic bomb to be used in warfare. The bomb exploded in the air five hundred and fifty metres above Hiroshima and it left seventy-eight thousand dead, eighty four thousand injured, and sixty thousand houses damaged or destroyed. A city had quite literally been wiped off the face of the earth by one bomb. Three days later a similar bomb was dropped on Nagasaki, and with this Japan finally lost the will to continue the war. Nine days after the first bomb had been dropped on Hiroshima, the Pacific War came to an end, slightly less than four years after the Japanese attack on Pearl Harbour.

It was the United States which developed the atomic bomb and which dropped it on Hiroshima and Nagasaki. The entire human race should have the terrible inferno that these bombs made of the two Japanese cities imprinted on its memory. Yet is it reasonable to heap criticism on the head of the United States alone? A number of countries had begun working on the development of atomic weapons in the 1940's, as is clear from the very fact that work in the United States was initially stimulated by similar work being undertaken in Germany. In Japan the army commissioned the Physical and Chemical Research Institute in 1941 to carry out research into the feasibility of atomic weapons, and by 1943 their work had reached the point of conducting experiments with concentrated uranium. If Japan had proved successful in developing atomic bombs first, the Japanese armed forces would almost certainly have used them. The fate of Hiroshima and Nagasaki might then have become the fate of San Francisco or London. What is important to remember is not so much which country was the first to use atomic bombs as the fact that any country that succeeded in developing them would have been sure to use them.

Death is still death, no matter whether it is brought about by a sword or by an atomic bomb. Given that the purpose of weapons is to kill and maim people, the difference between a sword and atomic bomb is not really one of kind. It is rather a difference of scale, of their power to kill people and of their efficiency as weapons. And it would seem to be precisely considerations such as these that have governed the so-called 'developments' in nuclear weaponry since Hiroshima. Following the United States, the Soviet Union succeeded in producing an atomic bomb in 1949, followed by Great Britain in 1952, France in 1960, the People's Republic of China in 1964 and India in 1974. And the United States, the Soviet Union and Great Britain have also successfully developed the much stronger hydrogen bomb as well. So long as it is true that the balance of power - or alternatively the balance of fear - is the factor that preserves our peace, then nuclear weapons can be expected to be a very efficient means of preserving peace.

Nonetheless, the emergence of nuclear weapons is responsible for the illogical bind that warfare has now reached. The logic of a balance of power based on an explicit nuclear strategy cannot avoid bringing mankind to the brink of extinction in the event of just one miscalculation. And it is by no means true that the leading countries in the art of warfare have always succeeded in keeping their military forces under the control of reason.

As a result of the two atomic bombs dropped on Hiroshima and Nagasaki, Japan has now withdrawn from warfare and the arms race. Japan may have the technology necessary to produce atomic weapons and may have the economic power to make them in large quantities, but it has nevertheless not turned itself into a nuclear power. The experience of Japan with atomic bombs has yet to bring forth any positive and determined approach to the problem of war, but it would appear to be clear that if the human race is

Atmic Bomb Dome

to have any future, some way must be found of getting beyond the belief that peace can only be preserved through possession of military might.

Hiroshima has now rebuilt. From the ashes of its destruction, it has grown now into a city with a population of 860,000. A city is of course more than just a collection of roads and buildings; it also represents the sum of the ideas and feelings of the people who live there. The Hiroshima that was physically destroyed will never therefore be erased from the consciousness of its citizens. The Hiroshima that has been resurrected in the post-war years stands on the same site as its predecessor, but it is twice the size. If the notion of civilization involves man's determination to make the most out of his life, then the rebuilding of Hiroshima can perhaps be said to be a symbol of the victory of civilization over the forces that destroyed it.

SONODA-Hidehiro

Dressing Like the West

Clothing which originally evolved in the Western European countries is today a common sight in virtually every country in the world, so universal phenomenon that one can easily overlook it. But why is it that these clothes have been so readily — and fully — accepted by peoples with quite different cultural affinities? In trying to find answers to these questions, a study of the history of Western clothing in Japan can prove extremely worthwhile.

Needless to say, the term "Western clothing" covers a wide range of apparel, and there have been many changes in fashion over the centuries. For instance, the tailcoat appeared sometime around 1810, the frock-coat in 1840, and the lounge suit after about 1850. But as can be seen from the above examples, when one talks of "Western clothing" in general, one is really referring to those fashions which evolved after the Industrial Revolution. The basic characteristics of such clothing can, on the other hand, be traced much farther back in history. The first time that the Japanese set eyes on Western clothes was in 1543 when a sailor was washed ashore from a Portuguese ship. Witnesses reported the absence of wide sleeves, as well as other features that differed from Japanese attire: the upper and lower halves were separated into jacket and trousers, the former being long, though not belted at the waist. It is a description that can be applied to the characteristics of most modern Western clothing.

Other foreigners visited the country during the sixteenth century, but it was not until after the arrival of Commodore Perry in 1853 — signalling the end of two and a half centuries of seclusion — that Japan's acquaintanceship with Western clothing really began. It was in 1855, that the bakufu government commenced a naval training programme at Nagasaki, in answer to the threat posed by the Americans. Here, for the first time, Western clothing was chosen by the Japanese; from then on it gradually grew in popularity, forming the uniforms of the armed forces. In 1870, the new government established after the Meiji Restoration decided on the official use of Western-style uniforms for messengers of the Council of State, and for both the army and the navy. At the same time, it was decreed that Western dress would replace traditional Japanese attire for those attending ceremonial events at the Imperial Palace. Thus, during the Meiji period (1868 – 1912), Western clothing came to be a symbol of high social station. But Western clothes spread gradually throughout Japanese society, being chosen for the uniforms of policemen and postmen, and for the sportswear and underwear of schoolchildren.

The reason for the popularity of Western apparel is that the Japanese appreciated its practicality; traditional Japanese clothes were, in contrast, recognized as being a constraint on the free movement of the body.

The process of acceptance so far outlined has been limited to men. The case of acceptance among women is somewhat different. Spending much of their lives in the home, Japanese women became acquainted with Western clothing in a manner quite unlike that already described. During the 1880s, the Japanese government was very concerned with trying to renegotiate the unequal treaties that had been signed with the Western powers in order to regain the right to decide its own tariffs and to abolish extraterritoriality. One condition for this was to win acceptance by the West, and it was therefore thought advantageous to display what would be regarded as proof that Japan was a "civilized" country. In 1883 the government erected the Rokumeikan, an elaborate hall for Western-style social functions attended by the elite of Japanese society and the diplomatic corps. Here, at the dances held every Sunday night, the bustle enjoyed a considerable following among the ladies who, like their male counterparts, had already begun wearing Western clothing at the Palace.

Turning to the other end of the social scale, those women who were engaged in manual labour during the latter half of the nineteenth century were mostly working on the land. Needless to say, a farmer demands that her working clothes be practical and functional. For generations, such people had worn jackets with tight sleeves and a type of trousers, thus enabling their limbs to move freely. There was no fundamental difference between these and Western clothes, and thus little incentive for Japanese women to change their clothing habits. The renowned scholar, Kon Wajirō (1888 – 1973), who founded the science of "modernology" once conducted some research into clothing trends which clearly illustrates this sex gap. The result of a survey he made in 1925 in Tokyo' s most famous shopping area, the Ginza, showed that 67% of men were wearing Western clothes, as compared to a mere 1% of women. A similar survey was repeated in exactly the same situation eight years later and, according to that, the percentage of females in Western clothes had risen to 19%; however, the majority of these were children and schoolgirls fitted out with Western-style uniforms. If only adult women were counted, the figure was still only 3%.

It was not until after the Second World War that Western clothing really became rooted in the lives of Japanese people. In fact, it has been so wholeheartedly adopted that nowadays traditional Japanese clothes have become a rare sight. Men have stopped wearing them, except perhaps when relaxing in the privacy of their own homes. The trend is even more noticeable among women; in general, the kimono is only worn for such formal occasions as weddings, funerals and graduation ceremonies. People have come to think of Japanese clothing as being a luxury: expensive and impractical. In contrast, Western clothing is usually practical and — when compared with Japanese clothing — relatively inexpensive.

Over the last century the Japanese have effected a considerable change in their clothing habits, switching over from traditional to Western styles. Over this same period, fashions in the West have become increasingly straightforward and simple. The same forces are at work in both East and West. The westernization of Japanese clothing habits is not so much a "victory" for a superior Western civilization, but rather a natural change in the modern world — with its emphasis on activity and practicality — which has evolved since the Industrial Revolution.

SONODA-Hidehiro

Radio and Television

The first television broadcast in Japan was transmitted from Tokyo at 2:00 PM on February 1, 1953. These were transmissions of NHK (the Japan Broadcasting Corporation, a broadcasting network financed partly by license fees). The receiver's fee was ¥200 per month, and at that time a total of 866 television sets were under contract. This initial 2:00 PM broadcast was of the network's opening ceremony, and featured a veteran announcer clad in formal dress complete with heavy makeup and painted-on eyebrows. Radio broadcasting had begun five years after the world premier broadcast from station KDKA in Pittsburgh, U.S.A. (November, 1920), with JOAK on March 3, 1925, and was followed by the births of BK Osaka in June, and Nagoya CK in July. NHK is the body which inherited this network, and in 1932 included 1 million contractees, growing to 6 million by 1941. Television broadcasting was then erected on this foundation. The atmosphere of the first broadcast was predictably tense: One episode which occurred was that the NHK Director, Furushio Tetsuro, suddenly forgot the name of one of his guests, the Governor of Tokyo Prefecture, and had to be prompted by the floor director.

Six months later, private networks also commenced broadcasting, and by the following year, transmissions were also being sent from Osaka and Nagoya.

The "tennis court romance" between the Crown Prince and Princess, and their subsequent marriage were reported by television, and in April, 1959, their betrothal parade was broadcast live nationwide. At this time, television sales soared radically, and it is said that all sets available, including those on display in show windows, were completely sold out. The first genuinely live broadcast was the hour and twenty-five minute coverage of the departure of the Crown Prince's ship from the port of Yokohama, on the occasion of his visit to the United Kingdom. Just as in the cases of Britain and Thailand, through the medium of television, the royal family of Japan has been able to win popularity with the broad masses of the citizenry. Even on a private network, there was a popular program entitled, "Royal Album".

In 1960, television entered the "color age". In this year, while the Japan Series was in progress, Chairman Asanuma of the Socialist Party was stabbed to death while giving a speech, and live action of the Series was interrupted in order to cover news of this terrorist act. By 1962, the number of NHK contractees broke through the 10 million mark, and NHK general broadcasting expanded to all-day transmission, starting at 6:25 AM and continuing until 11:50 PM. Contract agreements have kept increasing, topping 20 million sets in December, 1977, and reaching 30 million in September, 1982. If we also consider the television sets which are not under contract, we find that our figure nearly matches that of the 32 million households in Japan. Thus by calculating a total population of 101.4 million, we can see that there is one television set for every three people, or one for each household. In many regions, private networks provide at least four channels, and as many as nine or ten, some continuing coverage through the night, and during times of need, such as when a typhoon approaches, we are served by 24-hour broadcasting.

Such popularization of television has left a far-reaching impact on society. For one, political events can be broadcast nationwide as they occur. On November 23, 1963, the first attempt at satellite transmission between Japan and the United States was successful, but that initial report was of the assassination of President Kennedy, spreading a chill over the people. Other major incidents which were given full-scale coverage include the calling-in of security forces against students occupying Tokyo University's Yasuda Hall during the period of student uprisings in 1969, and the 10-hour coverage of the arrest of Red Army members at the Asama Villa in February, 1972.

There are, of course, major pre-arranged news broadcasts as well. Among these include coverage of the opening of the Tokaido New Trunk Line (Shinkansen) and the Olympics in 1964, the opening ceremony of the Osaka World Expo in 1970, simultaneous coverage of the Okinawa reversion treaty by satellite from Washington and Tokyo in 1971, and live coverage of the signing of the treaty of peace and friendship between Japan and China from Beijing in August, 1978. By satellite, television may be received instantaneously from almost anywhere in the world.

Series produced on location abroad are growing larger in scale. These began with the series, "Across the African Continent" in 1959, and in 1980, the "Silk Road" series, produced jointly by China and Japan, attracted great attention and popularity. Documentaries such as "Kanetaka Kaoru's World Travels", and "The Fabulous World Tour" are found on private networks.

The most popular programs on television, however, are entertainment shows, such as dramas, plays, music and variety shows. Sports also fall under this category. The national sport of sumo and "semi-national" sport of baseball (professional and high school) often succeed in focusing the nation's attention on the television screen. Among TV dramas, there are several which draw viewer ratings of over 50%. One percent equals 1.04 million citizens over seven years old, so 50% is over 50 million viewers. This medium, in which stars are born and then fade away, must be a universal phenomenon in this age of mass communications.

We can pose the question, however, as to whether Gresham's Law ("Mediocrity repels quality") also applies in the case of television programming. "TV children" (those deeply influenced by television) and the existence of poor quality late-night pornographic programs are widely criticized, but it still seems that Japanese television will continue to provide a rather high level of program quality in the future. Through the televised medium, we are able to enjoy classical arts such as Noh and Kabuki, as well as Western classical music, and works by Shakespeare. We might even say that, by means of the advanced technology of television, the traditions of Japanese craftsmen as well as those of performing artists are brought to life. In the future, taking into consideration the potentials offered by CATV and Character and Pattern Telephone Access Information Network (CAPTAIN) systems, we may look optimistically toward the future of the Japanese in the Television Era.

YONEYAMA-Toshinao

Cameras

The desire to retain the image of a loved one as a picture is probably common to everyone. In the eighth century, there was a soldier who was sent from the eastern provinces to the line of defense in the west and who wished to make a picture of his wife to gaze at along the way, but lamented that he had not even the time to do so. This is recorded in the *Man'yoshu*. Portrait art developed during the Mediaeval Age, when fine depictions of aristocrats, priests, and military leaders were produced. In the Tokugawa Period, Ukiyoe prints of actors by famous artisans sold well among the populace.

Thus this desire for portraits, going back to archaic times, changed to one for portrait photographs with the introduction of photography into Japan in the mid-nineteenth century. In the early Meiji Period, we can already find large numbers of photographs of faces, and records of everyday activities.

The impulse for recording is not limited to only people, of course, but applies also to scenes and events. We can find many examples of this as well in the history of Japanese art. Here this recording impulse and aesthetic sense come together, and, through the popularization of that instrument which combines the technologies of lens optics (a product of military origin) and mechatronics which is the camera, the Japanese today are among the most "photographic" of any people on earth. At least one camera is found in every home, and shutters click and flashes go off everywhere.

Photography, however, was originally highly

specialized skill. In towns and villages professional photographers opened up their studios and
took portraits on demand, or, when required,
went out to take commemorative photographs.
Daughters of marriageable age would don their
best clothing and have their portraits taken, which
would then be used by go-betweens as "bait" in
the selection of prospective spouses. The portrait
of the deceased on display at funerals has become a common practice. It is also not uncommon to see portrait photos of recent ancestors
hanging in the parlors of homes. Commemorative
photographs are taken upon entrance or graduation from school, and at weddings. The photo-
grapher became a specialist indispensable to the
town or village, just like a doctor or a dentist.

This profession still thrives, and such photographers are widely called upon for passport or
identification photos. However, we can now also
find many so-called "DPE" (developing, printing,
and enlarging) stores selling cameras and acces-
sories as well. Apart from those of the professional, the number of negatives and prints produced
by the one-camera-plus household is almost limit-
less. These DPE shops take care of their photo
needs. This trend has gotten even stronger since
the rise in popularity of color films.

"I can take pictures, too," is a commercial
catchphrase, and this reflects the fact that most
cameras are of the foolproof, "aim and shoot"
type. On the other hand, many people take pride
in possessing a camera with many interchange-
able lenses and other extras. Even for cameras
with simplified functions, consumers demand a
high degree of precision. For these reasons, both
the versatility of cameras and the systems for
handling film are improving.

Forest of various cameras (Kyodo)

So in a great variety of situations, fathers photograph their wives and children, mothers their babies, and children their parents and siblings. Albums accumulate pictures of the family. Such photographic energy is especially noticeable at various public occasions, so that rows of cameras at festivals are no longer a rarity.

This popularization of cameras is also reflected in the vividness of on-the-scene photos of fires or accidents. A record of tragedy is then possible. So, for the most part, it can be said that photography is the "Second Art", receiving wide acceptance from the masses. It is also said that with a camera, all Japanese become artists and poets. The existence of magazines and the formation of clubs by both professionals and amateurs corresponds to the situation for haiku and other forms of poetry, and photo exhibitions are held, just as for artists.

A technique related to that of the camera is moving pictures, or movies. An original form of this is found in the picture scrolls which developed in the twelfth century. These depicted stories of the foundation of shrines and temples, historical events such as the "Mongol Invasion Scroll", and also the "Tale of Genji Scroll". These scrolls are also valuable sources of information of life styles during this period.

This tradition later developed into the picture book and the picture play on the one hand, and is reflected in the movie on the other. This became an established form of popular entertainment in the Taisho period, but also gave birth to artists in the tradition of Noh and Kabuki, such as Kurosawa Akira, the film director.

As opposed to still photography, the production of films involves large sums of money. Thus we cannot say that film-making is a truly popular activity, but it also cannot be denied that there exists a relatively large group of would-be filmmakers. With the recent development and diffusion of video tape recording, the filming and handling of moving images has become easier, and we may very well now be witnessing the emergence of a new popular pastime.

Returning to the subject of the camera, we cannot ignore the great development of a new mode of journalism which centers on photographs and is an outgrowth of their wide acceptance. There are now weekly magazines which feature only photographs accompanied by short captions. The appearance of image media, led by photographs, as a counterpart to traditional print media, has led to a re-evaluation of our unwritten traditions.

YONEYAMA-Toshinao

The Motorization of Japan

Leaving aside the wind-powered or steam-powered vehicles in the early history of the motorcar, the first vehicles powered by an internal-combustion engine were the vehicles of the two Germans, G. Daimler and K. Benz, and the vehicle built by the Englishman, E. Butler, all of which first ran in 1885. In 1893 the American J. Ford succeeded in transforming gasoline into a fuel for the motorcar and in 1895 the first company for the production of cars was set up. By 1905 the Buick, Packard, Cadillac and Ford motorcar manufacturing companies were all in existence, along with many others in the United States, and the manufacture of cars powered by the internal-combustion engine had already made startling progress.

The first motorcar which was brought to Japan in 1899 was an American-made steam-powered car, the Rockomobile II Standard. Within just three years, by 1902, buses made in Japan with internal-combustion engines imported from the United States could be seen on the roads in Japanese cities, and by 1907 there was a fully-Japanese car in production, the Takuri, both the engine and the body of which were manufactured in Japan. It had a two-cylinder engine with a capacity of 1853cc and produced twelve horse-power. It was only later, around 1910, that the famous Model 'T' Ford was first imported to Japan.

Subsequently, Japanese manufacturers produced many different kinds of cars and it became fashionable and popular in the upper reaches of society to have a motorcar for private use. Mass-production of Japanese-made cars began in 1914 with the Datto, a car manufactured by the Kaishinsha Company for some two to three years: its name means 'tremendous speed'. The Datto had a ten horse-power engine, three forward gears and one reverse gear, and, except for the tires, the magneto and the spark plugs, was produced entirely in Japan. In 1917, with financial assistance from the government of the day, the Kaishinsha Company turned to the production of vehicles for military use, but it went bankrupt during the depression of the years 1924-25.

The Great Earthquake of 1923 destroyed all the electric trams running in Tokyo. To cope with the sudden transportation problems, large numbers of Model 'T' Ford lorries were hastily ordered from the United States and were used as buses, thus bringing the ordinary Japanese into contact with motorized vehicles perhaps for the first time.

Production of Japanese-made cars was unable, however, to keep pace with demand, and so in 1924 and 1925 plants were established in Japan for assembling Ford cars and the General Motor's Chevrolet respectively. By 1929 some thirty thousand foreign vehicles were being assembled in Japan each year, while during the same year the production of Japanese vehicles came to a mere 437 units. But one by one the Tokyo Jidosha (later known as Isuzu), Nissan and Toyota companies started manufacturing cars. And, owing to the imposition of customs dues designed to help Japanese manufacturers establish themselves in the market and to foreign exchange controls, the assembly of foreign cars came to an end in 1939. By 1941 the three Japanese companies just referred to were producing between them forty thousand vehicles a year, but air raids had put an end to their production by the time of Japan's surrender in August 1945. During the years of the Occupation, which was symbolized by the jeeps used by the United States Forces in Japan, cars gradually reappeared on Japan's roads.

After the war, the three pre-war companies were joined by Toyo Industries, Fuji Heavy Industries, Honda, Mitsubishi and other new manufacturers of cars. But the era of the car really only came to Japan in the nineteen-sixties. Mass-production of vehicles in Japan encountered a number of problems in the early post-war years but these were mostly overcome by the sixties. In 1965 the Meishin Expressway connecting Kobe and Nagoya was opened. Since then a number of other expressways have been constructed and Japan had now three thousand kilometres of expressway, with plans for more to be built bringing the total up to 7600 kilometres by the twenty-first century. Also during the sixties, rapid progress was made with paving roads throughout the country, even in remote areas.

Keeping pace with all these developments have been changes in the design of cars and increases in the number of vehicles produced each year. In 1960, 760,000 units were produced, but ten years later in 1970 the total was 5,300,000, a staggering increase of almost 700 per cent. In 1980 the total reached eleven million, which was more than the total number of vehicles produced in the United States in that year.

In 1964 the word 'motorization' became a popular word, indicating the shift to a motorized society. At the end of 1979 there was a total of 350 million cars and other vehicles in the world. Of this total, more than 154 million (45%) were in the United States, more than 37 million (11%) were in

Japan, and more than 24 million (7%) were in West Germany, so it is clear that Japan has indeed become a motorized society. Furthermore Japanese cars, with their small size, low fuel consumption and high quality are selling well in Europe and America, but this is provoking a considerable amount of friction between Japan and its trading partners.

The influence of the motorcar on society has been various. People have acquired much more freedom of movement than they used to enjoy and the geographical area they cover in their daily lives have undergone considerable expansion, too. Those with cars have found themselves particularly welcome in country areas. The spread of the car has been even more remarkable in country areas than in the cities, and it is now quite common for country households to have two or even three vehicles. On the other hand, though, traffic accidents have been increasing rapidly, too, and in 1970 as many as 16,800 people were killed in traffic accidents. Since that year the figure has gone down somewhat, but it still stands at between eleven and thirteen thousand deaths per year. There are also mountains of discarded cars all over Japan, an obvious symbol of great waste.

Japanese cars are now being exported all over the world. They can be seen in Africa, in the Middle East and in South-East Asia as well as in Europe and America, and they seem to enjoy great popularity. They are for the most part, however, small-sized cars clearly reflecting the fact that they are the products of a country in which space is at a premium.

YONEYAMA-Toshinao

Computers and Robots

The old man went to the mountain to cut kindling, and the old woman went to the river to do the laundry--the fairy tale, "The Peach Lad", opens with this mention of the division of labour: the old woman then finds a peach floating downstream, from which the Peach Lad is born.----And so the story goes. Aside from the story's plot, however, the scene of laundry being done at the riverbank is one which was by no means unusual even half a century ago in Japan.

Now, however, clothes are laundered in a fully automatic clothes washer. By merely filling the machine with laundry and soap, and pressing the button determining washing program, the machine fills with water, and clothes are washed, rinsed, drained and finally spun dry.

Cooking, as well as laundering is also automated. The rice cooker complete with timer is well-known, but other automated items include the cooking range, dishwasher, and dishdryer.

Sewing machines now are equipped with a variety of built-in programs, and those which have adjustable sewing styles are widely used. Cameras, VTRs, and record players now also incorporate similar electronic mechanisms.

When we step outside our homes, we meet electronic gates at stations, "on-line" systems of banking automation, and alcohol or cigarette vending machines. Telephones and mail sorting are also automated. Automobiles now contain many automatic features, and the railroad system from the "Bullet Train" on down utilize ATC, (Automatic Train Control), making the engineer next to unnecessary. Today we find office auto-

Automatic ticket taken at railway station

mation (OA) on centre stage. Vocational high schools have instituted courses in computers, and computer training courses of all types are being set up everywhere.

The factory also has a new face: on the assembly line, robots are at work alongside humans. Many tasks involving painting, welding, and assembling have passed from human hands to robots, and inspection and measurement robots are also on the job. There are 67 thousand robots in operation in Japan (1981 figures), accounting for 70 percent of all in use in the world. Furthermore, Japan leads the world in robot production with 20 thousand units produced yearly. This trend is found not only in the large-scale manufacturers, but smaller subcontractors and local plants are also introducing more and more robots into their labour force.

"Mechatronics", a term coined in Japan from the combination of the two English words, mechanism and electronics, is used as the generic term for this technology: this refers to machines and tools which embody micro-computers in their mechanisms.

The development of this new technical array, represented by computers and robots, is also called a "new industrial revolution" and is composed of the merger of innovations in several fields.

The integrated circuit (IC), which reduced the size of what we now think of as the mammoth vacuum tube computer, paved the way for the large-scale integrated circuit (LSI), and then for very large-scale integration. The raw materials start with silicon, to which are added all types of ceramics, liquid crystals, light fibers, lasers, magnetics, active molecules, germanium, brought together by the application of electrical engineering theory. The improvement of sensors corresponding to our five senses, and more efficient motors are also important. To this we add continual progress in fine technology.

The skill of the Japanese in detailed handiwork is often given as the factor making possible this advanced technology, but we might more correctly view this wave of innovation as deriving not from innate sources, but rather originating from the "system" of Japanese civilization. A social structure based on consideration of others and a delicate sensitivity toward beauty are characteristics of this civilization.

The danger of unemployment caused by increasing introduction of robots and automation is being raised as a danger by some critics, and in Europe innovations are being stifled because of labour union opposition. In Japan, however, the fact that technical innovation does not directly lead to higher unemployment owing to the social makeup has facilitated this revolution up to this time.

The continual development of this advanced technology as the world moves into the 21st century has been expressed in such terms as "the third wave" (Toffler) and "megatrends" (Nesbits), and Japan is considered as one of the front-runners among developed nations. The Japanese animistic or pantheistic world view has been identified as a factor weakening resistance to the technology which usurps religious authority: but a kind of idolatry also exists which we may call "techno-animism". We must not forget that the urge to return to nature, and to protect nature has been expressed in the rise of movements against nuclear weapons, nuclear war, and the development of nuclear energy sources.

YONEYAMA-Toshinao

The Home

In the nearly forty-year interval since the last war, the substance of modern-day family life has undergone dramatic changes. This fact is certainly apparent in the relationships between different family members: husband and wife, parents and children, brother and sister, and wife and mother-in-law. Family size has in fact dropped, from an average of five before the war to just over three today. Cases of single child families are also rising in number. The patriarchal, primogeniture male-oriented system of the Meiji constitution has given way to a new, post-war constitution and civil law which recognizes equality of rights between the sexes, and to improvement in the status of women.

An even clearer transformation can be seen, however, in the material foundation upon which the home is built; that is, the goods necessary for carrying on our daily lives. This does not refer only to the so-called 'new towns', which are new living environments springing up everywhere. In the older cities as well, the ravages of wartime bombings have paved the way for wider streets, and sewage systems where there had been none before. Also, the 'urbanization' phenomenon has led to changes in the ways of life in the farming, mountain, and fishing villages as well. One cause for this is found in the changeover of farmers and fishermen to urban patterns of labour, but we should recognize that the most striking element of change here is to be found in the rapid economic growth which began in about 1958 and lasted until the oil shock of 1973.

In rural villages until around 1957, inhabitants

still used wood-burning ovens and charcoal. Water was drawn from wells by hand pumps, and in the northeastern prefectures, wood-burning hearths were found in living rooms. Electric lighting and radio were available, but television was still a rarity. Yet just ten years later, in these same villages, nearly all houses were equipped with television, electric clothes washers, electric pumps (or running water), propane gas ranges, microwave ovens, and refrigerators. All homes possessed telephones and cars. When the same goods as were found in the city became available in the country as well, rural homes came to be even more well off than their urban counterparts.

Possession of electric appliances for the Japanese home became one of the measures of industrial growth. If count is made of the electric motors in each home, the results will be surprising: washing machines, sewing machines, record

Kitchen fully equipped with electric appliances

players, tape recorders, electric shavers, and countless electric toys. Timers for rice cookers, thermostats for air conditioners, and the housewife's answer to the abacus, the electronic calculator, are also examples of the appearance of electronics in the home.

In the home of the past, such chores as cooking, cleaning, and laundry were the province of the woman of the house, and unless she could afford to have a hired help attend to these tasks, it was the rule that her hands would suffer. Most of this work has been facilitated by machines today, and women's hands are more beautiful for it.

In 1974-75, a group of researchers conducted a survey of the household goods found in 140 apartments ranging from the "2K" type (two bedrooms plus kitchen) to the "5DK" type (five bedrooms plus dining room/kitchen) in the eastern and western metropolitan districts. The results of this showed that, of the homes studied, the home with the most goods had a total of 1178 items, while that with the least had 460 items. 31.4% of homes contain between 800 and 899 items while 74.3% contained goods in the 700 to 999 item range. In other words, 70% of families living in apartments possess between 700 and 1000 household goods. It goes without saying that for families living in the same place over an extended period of time, the number of possessions grow. According to another survey, at a certain Sado fishing village, it became known that a total of 6500 items were counted in a certain residence and storehouse, and that, of these, only about 20% were employed in daily use.

People who have considered the home through a detailed examination of its contents have made several notable discoveries.

First of all, most of the large furniture to be found in a typical apartment was obtained by the wife at the time of her wedding, as her "trousseau".

Secondly, in virtually all homes, we can find a washing machine, a refrigerator, a vacuum cleaner, a low "foot-warming" table, a rice cooker, a steam iron, and a power sewing machine. All of these electric appliances are designed as labour-savers for the housewife.

In these modern homes, there is no formal parlour. Reception of guests, weddings, funerals, and the like are nearly all handled outside the home, and eating out has also increased. The sales of food service industries is at a yearly level of ¥16 trillion.

Housekeeping and etiquette which were traditional in the home have now lost their place and times. The schedules of the various family members have become individualized, and opportunities for family togetherness are few and far between.

The woman is still the centre of the home today, and around the mother and child axis, interior decoration is accomplished by the introduction of various ornaments. The man is excluded from this process.

In this manner, when judged by its contents, the Japanese home has been blessed with abundance. Closets, sewing machines, dressing tables, televisions, and dolls are present in every home, no matter what the size. Interiors brim with a jumble of things, but lack the space to store them. On top of this, many of these things have a story or memory to go with it.

YONEYAMA-Toshinao

Coping with Energy Problems

With the coming of the fourth Middle-East War in November 1973, the arab nations made use of an 'oil strategy', which resulted in a boycott of petroleum exports to enemy states, and delivery limitations to unfriendly nations, thus bringing about the so-called 'oil shock'. In Japan this situation led to shortages of goods due to hoarding by housewives; service stations closing on holidays, prices skyrocketting, and local savings banks being hit by mass withdrawals. In early 1974 the reduction of power, and energy conservation, typified by reduced broadcast time by the NHK television network, the curtailing of lights and neon by department stores, became the rule. That year saw a bad economic climate consisting of price fluctuations, bankruptcies, and negative economic growth.

It can be claimed that the Japanese were not aware of the energy crisis until after they had experienced this nightmare. Subsequently, the International Energy Association (INA), an organization of consumer nations directed against the OPEC members, came into being, and the Japanese were able to ameliorate the effects of the oil shock. Since then, while achieving only modest economic growth, Japan alone has succeeded in continuing to maintain a favourable economic climate.

No one can deny that Japan now enjoys great prosperity. In industrial production, this prosperity is supported by a high level of technology. However, if one takes a hard look at reality, one must admit that this prosperity is erected on an unstable foundation — a house built on sand.

Japan's industry today is dependent on imports for the fulfilment of eighty-nine per cent of its energy requirements, and seventy-five per cent of this is supplied by petroleum. Furthermore, eighty per cent of Japan's petroleum supplies comes from the Middle East (1977 figures). Domestically-produced energy stands only at 11 per cent of Japan's energy requirements - it consists of coal, nuclear power, and hydro-electric power, while domestic petroleum, natural gas and wood providing less than one per cent of the total.

Dependence on petroleum is so great that we call civilization today the 'oil culture'. Japan is no exception, and the rapid growth of the heavy chemical industry from petroleum refineries has created even greater demands for oil. If oil imports, which amount to seventy-five per cent of Japan's energy requirements, were to be cut off, the Japanese economy would crumble immediately. One writer has calculated that if no supplies of oil reached Japan from the Middle East for two hundred days, three million people would die and seventy per cent of the nation's wealth would be lost.

World demand for crude oil and low growth rates have both improved since the days following the oil shock, so the atmosphere of crisis has somewhat diminished. The underlying problems, however, have not changed in the slightest.

Warnings of a limit to the world's petroleum resources were lacking before 1973, but they came to be fully appreciated after the oil shock. This was clearly seen in the hoarding by housewives. The very sensitivity of the reaction in resource-poor Japan may itself be useful for the future.

Many visions of life in the twenty-first century are being put forward by the government and by private researchers alike, but the one point all of these plans share is their recognition of the importance to Japan of an energy policy. In *Japan in the Year 2000*, a report compiled by the Long-Range Forecasting Committee of the Economic Planning Agency's Economic Council, the compilers state that, 'The energy situation for 1981-82 showed a transition to a state of relative stability, but the long-term energy outlook remains one of instability'. Also, 'the appearance of man-made fuels and new energy sources on the market will not come until the twenty-first century, and alternative sources such as nuclear power, coal and natural gas will not be competitive with oil until at least well into the 1990s'. This 'energy gap', which will continue until the development of alternative sources of energy, will mean, according to the report, that Japan, as a country with a high rate of petroleum imports, will continue to be faced with threats to its economic safety.

Spurred on by the oil crisis, Japan's efforts in the direction of energy conservation have continued to make rapid progress. Over the past ten years, energy-saving techniques have managed to conserve roughly twenty per cent of total con-

Tsuruga Nuclear Power Plant (The Kansai Electric Power Co., Ltd.)

sumption: by the year 2000, seventy-three per cent of present-day energy consumption can be saved.

The report mentioned above predicts that in the future it will be impossible to restrict demands of petroleum to the present level, which now amount to five million barrels a day, and that it will be necessary to continue to develop coal, nuclear power, natural gas, liquified coal, fuel alcohols, and solar energy. Finally, it declares that the main goals of an energy policy should be the development of a diversity of energy sources, further progress in energy conservation, and oil stockpiling.

In *The Task for Japan* (1978), a report which was compiled by the NIRA, a comprehensive research and development organization, there is some stress on the importance, for a society of few natural resources like Japan, of shifting from an abundance of goods to an abundance of spiritual values. This report states that, ' Through the entire course of our history, the present gaudy, obnoxious, materialistic civilization has existed only for twenty or thirty years, which amounts to little more than an instant when compared with a long history that has been characterized by a continuing search for spiritual worth' . The declaration that a return to spiritual abundance is the greatest contribution that Japan could make to world civilization is based on a conviction that reaches to the heart of the energy crisis.

YONEYAMA-Toshinao

Imitators or Innovators?

The climax of Akira Kurosawa's film Kage-musha is the scene of the battle of Nagashino, which took place in 1575. It faithfully depicts the defeat and retreat of the mounted knights from the east under the command of Takeda Katsuyori before the firepower of the matchlock-men of the combined western armies of Oda Nobunaga and Tokugawa Ieyasu. It was a symbolic battle, for it marked a turning point in the progress from ideas of warfare based on mounted knights to the new strategies offered by firepower.

Firearms first reached Japan in 1543, when they were brought ashore on the island of Tanegashi-ma off the south coast of Kyushu. It was not long before Japan was making her own firearms, and these played an important part in the battle of Nagashino. Shortly thereafter, Oda Nobunaga managed to unite the entire country under his rule, but behind his success lay revolutions in warfare, brought about by the introduction of firearms to Japan, and in castle architecture.

The story of how firearms were imported to Japan and how Japanese were soon inspired to produce similar weapons is one that shows the skill and speed of the Japanese at copying or imitating technological innovations. It is now something of an international truism that the Japanese are good copiers. And it would seem to be the case that many Europeans and Americans who feel threatened by the speed and skill of Japanese technological assimilation view the Japanese skill at copying and imitation with ill favour.

An American anthropologist has written an essay entitled 'One Hundred Percent American'. In it he used a number of concrete examples to show that almost all the things used or worn by people who think themselves to be totally American were from outside the United States. The elements of both material and spiritual culture, after all, move freely from culture to culture and country to country and the pattern of copying and imitation is common to all countries.

In the paintings of Picasso and Braque the influence of African art can be discerned, but, as is well known, the works of Van Gogh and the other impressionists reveal the influence of the Japanese ukiyo-e prints quite clearly. Going even further back, the Kakiemon ware of Arita in Kyushu reached Europe and created kilns in Meissen near Dresden. Thus Japanesque has a long history as an undercurrent in the history of European art.

Since the Japanese archipelago was situated on the eastern borders of the area covered by Chinese civilization, Japan has from the earliest times learnt, copied and absorbed much from the Chinese. In particular, during the Chinese T'ang dynasty (618–907), Japanese copied the plan according to which the T'ang capital, Ch'ang-An, had been built and used the same grid-iron scheme both for Heijo-kyo, the early eighth century capital near present-day Nara, and for Heian-kyo, the late eighth century capital in what is now Kyoto. Confucianism, Buddhism, and the Chinese writing system were also introduced to Japan at that time and had a part to play in the formation of the early Japanese state.

Now the reverse is happening of course, as words coined in Japan to translate words from Western languages are being adopted into the Chinese language and becoming widely used.

One example is the word 'tetsugaku', coined in Japan as an equivalent for the word 'philosophy'.

The next experience Japan had of influence from abroad was the introduction from Western Europe in the sixteenth century of Christianity and firearms, which have been discussed earlier. From the beginning of the seventeenth century, however, Japan adopted a policy of national seclusion and the succeeding (Pax Tokugawa) lasted for some two hundred years. The next changes came with the Meiji Restoration of 1868. After 1868, Japan modelled its constitution and army on those of Prussia, its trade practices and navy on those of England, and its technology and democracy on those of America. In these ways Japan 'copied' aspects of each of these countries.

It should be noted that while Japan did indeed copy from other countries, it did not either rest content with what it had copied or simply preserve what it had copied in its original form. Thus while adopting the basic grid-iron plan of Ch'ang-An, the early capitals also developed neighbourhood communities based on the street or the block as units. The T'ang system of laws and ordinances was also modified to make it fit more closely with the Japanese circumstances to which it was to be applied: by the thirteenth century Japan also had a system of laws for the military houses which had grown up alongside the T'ang laws and ordinances to give the Japanese state a dual structure. In the Meiji period the already much-transformed T'ang system underwent a modern transformation, and then finally there were further changes after Japan's defeat in the Second world War.

The same is true of Japan's adaptation of new technologies: Japan has not simply followed the technological path taken by more advanced countries, but has also added new elements of its own to the received technologies, and this is one of the features of modern Japan.

Some people say that the ideas contained in the special short form of Japanese poetry called the haiku are similar to those of Chinese poets and therefore that the haiku lacks originality or creativity. But this could only be said by someone who was ignorant of the fact that the Japanese poetic technique of honkadori, whereby the words, ideas, or themes of the works of earlier poets are used in new poems, is an important part of Japanese cultural life. In foreign countries, too, it has long been the custom for men and women of discernment to quote well-known sayings or poems.

Some people insist upon drawing a distinction between originals and copies, but there can be no doubt that the culture of mass society today owes a good deal to copying techniques, reproductions and replicas. It is through reproductions that we can come close to the finest works of art, and it is, for example, through photographs that we can get to know the reliefs on the Acropolis.

It should be recognized that copying in its various forms has served to raise the level of human culture as a whole. Without copying, it would have been impossible for culture to have attained global spread it has now. Nobody would deny that potatoes and corn are now crops that cover the world, even though they may orignally have come from the New World. Similarly, the arts and crafts of Japan, including the products of modern technology such as electrical appliances and motorcars, are now parts of global culture.

YONEYAMA-Toshinao

Police and Crime

Dotted throughout Japan are a large number of police boxes familiarly known as 'kōban'. The word 'kōban' was coined in the early Meiji period when a modern police force was established in Japan and it referred to a place where policemen took it in turns to be on duty.

In the ninth chapter of his book, *Japan As Number One*, Professor Ezra Vogel takes up the question of crime prevention in Japan. He points out that there is a network of some five thousand eight hundred 'kōban' throughout the cities of Japan protecting the hundred million city-dwellers of Japan from crime. In country districts there are police substations for every five thousand people and there are some ten thousand of these substations throughout the country. Owing to the high density of Japan's population, he reminds readers, the area covered by each police box or substation is quite small.

The title of this book is obviously one that tends to make the Japanese feel self-satisfied, but he wrote it mainly with American readers in mind. A sociologist by profession, he based his arguments on hard facts and discussed areas where he thought America could learn from Japan. People say that Tokyo is a city where a woman can walk alone even at the dead of night and be safe. Professor Vogel's book seeks to publicize the secrets of the high level of public order that is to be found in Japan and that is epitomized by the safety of one of the world's largest cities.

According to the statistics published for the year 1973, the rate for any category of crime is at least four times as high in the United States as it is in Japan. For murders the figure is more than four times, for rape it is five times, and for robbery it is one hundred and five times as high. Furthermore, since the rate of reporting crimes is higher in Japan than in the United States, these figures if anything underestimate the differences in the crime rates of the two countries.

Japan enjoys not only a low crime rate, but also a high arrest rate for those crimes that are committed. In 1974, for example, the arrest rate was only 22 per cent in the United States but 69 per cent in Japan. For crimes of violence it is particularly high, standing at 96 per cent for murders, 93 per cent for causing bodily harm, 86 per cent for arson, and 83 per cent for rape.

As one of the reasons he puts forward to explain the successful control of crime in Japan, Professor Vogel points to the willingness of people to inform the police of any trouble, relying on the emergency number 110 which can be used anywhere in Japan and is known to everybody. And then there is the fact that the average time taken for a policeman to reach the scene at which his presence is required is only three minutes and twenty-three seconds, and also the network of 'kōban' mentioned above. He points out that the police in the local 'kōban' keep in close touch with the people residing in their area and know everything about them from the number of people in each family to the kinds of valuables they have in their possession. He says that the local inhabitants recognize the need for the police to collect information of this kind and therefore cooperate willingly with the police.

Other factors that make it easier for crime to be successfully controlled include the existence of a uniform body of law on the basis of which the police in all the prefectures of Japan can readily cooperate with one another. There is no question, he points out, of fleeing to another prefecture to escape the rigors of the law. And since the crime rate is itself low, large numbers of policemen can be mobilized to work on a single crime.

Vogel also gives some emphasis to the sense of professionalism the Japanese police have. Whereas American policemen are trained for just eight weeks, in Japan it takes a year to train a policeman and there is a centralized education system for the higher ranks too. And since they are concentrated in small groups they have the sense of being comrades and are not so conscious of vertical relations between the different ranks. As a result they have a strong sense of group loyalty and this engenders a high level of morale. They are allowed some measure of initiative in dealing with individual problems, but specialists are assigned to deal with crimes as they occur. Drunkenness and gambling are treated indulgently so long as nobody is harmed in the process. Anything but indulgence is shown to those involved in the cultivation, manufacture, smuggling, sales or use of drugs, or to those involved in traffic accidents or infringements of the traffic regulations. Traffic regulations in Japan are strict, and cover not only such matters as speed limits and drunken driving, but also licences and the state of maintenance of cars on the road.

Other factors Vogel draws attention to are the cooperative bonds between the 'kōban' and their neighbourhoods based on their everyday contact with the local residents, and the self-control exercised by people as members of a locality so as to avoid doing anything that might disturb neighbourhood relations. Also he points out that the police work hard to maintain their good reputation and thus use public opinion to work in their favour.

The writer of a book comparing the Japanese and the Jews made the interesting observation in it that the Japanese think that their water and their safety are free. The author poses as a Jew, but it is widely supposed that this is just a mask and that the Japanese who appears as the supposed translator is in fact the real author.

Japan currently still maintains strict control over the possession of knives and guns and most people regard it as a matter of course that Japan is an unarmed society. But in fact this tradition goes back to 1588, when Toyotomi Hideyoshi organized a sword hunt to remove swords from those not entitled to wear them, and it was reinforced after the Meiji Restoration by the government ban on the wearing of swords. So the policy has long been that people are to go about unarmed, with the exception in the Edo period of the samurai and in modern times of the regular army and police officers. It is true that there were large numbers of samurai in the Edo period but it has to be remembered that most had bureaucratic functions and their swords served merely as part of their official dress. So it should perhaps be said that law and order in Japan have a tradition that goes back four hundred years to the time when the bearing of arms ceased to be recognized as a right.

YONEYAMA-Toshinao

Security through Diplomacy

The beginnings of Japanese diplomacy are to be found in an exchange of greetings between Prince Shotoku (593-621) and Emperor Sui of China in the seventh century. Japan in those days had been organized as a state under the overwhelming influence of Chinese civilization, taking from it its political administration, its arts and sciences, its religion, its technology, and so on. Nevertheless it was not long before these imports underwent some Japanization and stress came to be placed in time on the Japanese originality which had led to the changes. Thus the native religion was brought under the influence of Buddhism and Taoism and systematized, and Shinto was the result. Similarly, the Kana signs, which are a syllabary used to represent the sounds of the Japanese language, have their origin in abbreviated forms of the Chinese characters introduced from China. Consciousness of Japanese originality in these areas led to the emergence of the expectation that Japan would be able to maintain equal relations with its diplomatic partners. Such a pattern has been repeated time and again in the long course of Japan's history.

In 1854 the Edo bakufu concluded the Treaty of Kanagawa, a treaty of friendship between the United States and Japan, in response to American demands for the opening of Japanese ports to foreign trade. Subsequently the bakufu concluded similar treaties with England, Russia, the Netherlands, and France. These treaties, however, allowed not only for the opening of the ports and free trade, but also consular jurisdiction (extraterritoriality) and foreign settlement concessions. They were unequal treaties because Japan could neither alter nor revise them on its own authority and because Japan had no autonomy in the matter of levying customs dues. These circumstances aroused national passions and reinforced feelings of nationalism, with the result that a movement emerged which was dedicated to reverence for the emperor and the expulsion of the barbarians, as the foreigners were termed. This was one of the factors which eventually led to the fall of the Tokugawa government.

After the Meiji Restoration in 1868, the government even went to the extent of bringing Japanese customs and habits closer to those of the West in the hope of getting the Western nations to agree to revision of the treaties, but it was not in fact until 1911, well after Japan's victory in the Russo-Japanese War, that Japan was able to gain new treaties with the Western powers that conferred on it the status of a diplomatic equal.

After 1945 Japan was for several years under American occupation as a defeated nation, but in 1951, at the San Francisco Peace Conference, Japan concluded a peace treaty with the forty-eight participating nations. In 1956 diplomatic relations with the Soviet Union were restored and Japan was admitted to the United Nations. In 1972 diplomatic relations with the People's Republic of China were restored, and in 1978 a treaty of peace and friendship was concluded between China and Japan. Thus little by little Japan extended the circle of its diplomatic relations with all the countries of the world.

Ever since Shotoku Taishi's diplomacy of the seventh century, complicated diplomatic protocol and ceremony have been a part of Japan's diplomatic relations. Politicians, high-ranking offi-

cials and the imperial family too all have important roles to play in the protocol of diplomatic relations. Heads of state who come to Japan on
official visits are invited to the Imperial Palace
and accommodated in the Official Guest House,
which was modelled on the Palace of Versailles.
In all countries there are Japanese embassies and
consulates and in each of them can be seen the
glitter of the gold imperial crest, a sixteen-
petalled chrysanthemum. Many of Japan's diplomatic customs follow the style established by
the absolute monarchies of Europe in the
nineteenth century: this is a curious fact, but it is
probably the same the world over. Japan is in
fact one of the countries in which most attention
is paid to diplomatic ritual.

In recent years there have been some special
trends in Japanese diplomacy. After the Second
World War Japan's diplomacy was criticized as
being in line with that of the United States or
'thoroughly pro-American', on account of Japan's
consciousness of its close relationship with America. But in 1972, after President Nixon's visit to
China in 1971, Japan restored its relations with
China; in 1973 it made diplomatic efforts to come
closer to the Arab countries; in 1975 Japan recognized North Vietnam; in 1977 it established three
fundamental principles to be followed in its relations with the countries of South-East Asia (1/
That Japan will be a peaceful country and will not
become a military state; 2/ That political, economic and cultural exchange will be carried out on a
basis of mutual trust; and 3/ That they will
cooperate as equal partners); in 1978 Japan concluded a peace treaty with China; and in 1979 an
economic summit was held in Tokyo. Thus bit by
bit Japan has pressed ahead with its own di-

284 Security through Diplomacy

plomatic initiatives. Nowadays Japan's foreign policy is based on friendship with America and with the advanced countries of Europe, but Japan's diplomatic policy as a whole is to maintain friendly relations with all countries. As a state Japan has renounced war in its constitution and is dependent for its survival on trade, so it must pursue a foreign policy of mutual security which is based not just on defense but also on economic assistance and careful diplomacy. Japan has not got a long tradition of skillful diplomacy, but in the midst of the trade fricitions and complicated international relations that beset the world now, she has no alternative but to continue to strive to avoid situations where Japan could become a cause of tension and conflict.

YONEYAMA-Toshinao

Tax and Social Welfare

One of the earliest recorded political upheavals in Japan is a court coup d'état that occurred in the year 645 A.D. known as the Taika Reforms. Based on the continental model of centralized government, these reforms placed both land and people under the direct control of the state: all land became part of the public domain, and all inhabitants became citizens of the state. The country was divided systematically into provinces, which were further subdivided into districts and villages. Furthermore, a taxation system was instituted, modelled on the Chinese system and consisting of three basic elements. The first of these was in effect a land tax; rice lands were supposed to be allotted to all citizens over the age of six, the area depending on whether the person was male or female, freeman or slave. The second was a labour tax, or corvée, although it could be paid in the form of textiles and other goods. And the third was a produce tax, to be paid in kind with the particular produce of the region.

This ancient system of taxation has continued down to the present day, and even the name of the government organ which oversees it, the Ōkura-shō, still exists. Needless to say, the taxes themselves are not the same, but the basic principle - that those in power use their power to extract property from the populace in order that they may maintain that same power - remained unchanged up until the Meiji Restoration of 1868. Even then, the right to collect taxes which had been exerted by the feudal lords during the Edo period (1600 - 1867) was merely passed on to the new Meiji government. Consequently it is not surprising that in the new Meiji Constitution there was little emphasis on the rights of the taxpayer.

Having issued a great number of national bonds in an effort to make up for shortfalls in revenue, however, the government has been courting bankruptcy and is now anxious to carry out reforms in the taxation system. What might be called 'fine tuning' has been carried out using, for instance, the commodity tax on luxury goods and the road tax levied on car owners, but there is strong opposition to any possible introduction of a large indirect tax. At the same time, there are complaints of unfairness with regard to the taxation of salaried workers, whose income is the most easy to ascertain and tax; in comparison, the self-employed and farmers have a much greater opportunity for hiding part of their incomes. It is true that occasionally tax frauds are exposed, but generally speaking, one can say that the Japanese are honest when it comes to paying their taxes.

Tax money is, of course, used by the state and local authorities for the necessary functioning of their administration such as the construction of roads, bridges and railways, the operation of the educational system, the promotion of various industries, the maintenance of public peace and order, defense, and so on. One expenditure which has become a considerable problem in recent years is the ballooning welfare budget. This has been criticized as the legacy of lavish welfare spending, overgenerous payments made during the period of rapid economic growth in the 1960's. No doubt what spurs people to make such criticisms is the realization that Japanese society is slowly but surely ageing.

Although there may be some people who assert

that Japan's social welfare is the best in the world, a recent government report states that the ratio between social security benefits and national income will reach the level of those of Western Europe only by the 21st century. Social security for medical expenses is fairly generous, and some take the view that this is what is responsible for the steady increase in life expectancy among the Japanese. It is certain that from now on, however, Japan will become a country in which the aged account for an increasingly large segment of the population, and one which requires support. Consequently many feel that the burden of large welfare budgets is inescapable.

At the same time there is also the view that taxes in Japan are very low when compared with those in other countries. If, for instance, one calculates a country's tax revenues as a percentage of its GDP (Gross Domestic Product), one finds that in 1976 the figure for Sweden was highest at 50.89%, followed by France with 39.11%, Great Britain with 37.35%, West Germany with 36.38%, the U.S.A. with 29.57%, and Japan with an extremely low 21.33%. Some people therefore think that taxes can be raised still more.

If one thinks back to the past, one can say that welfare in Japan used to be supported by both the family system and the traditional village community. The aged, the widows and the orphans were either looked after by relatives, or failing that by members of the local community. It is because this role has been gradually taken over by local and central government that tax revenue is now required to perform the same service to society. It cannot be denied that, in one sense, this change has been accompanied by a cooling of the once warm relationships that bound people together. However, times change and there is little one can do about it.

At present various administrative reforms are being discussed with a view to finally pulling the national finances out of the red. The ideal behind these moves is so-called "cheap government". It is certainly true that, with the present bureaucratic system, there exist a number of old-fashioned organs of the government which serve little purpose today. On the other hand, one should be aware that over the last century the investment and financing carried out by the government has clearly served to stimulate the economy of Japan. . One would hope that the reformers, in trying to effect a cure, do not make the mistake of killing the goose that lays the golden eggs.

In the past it may have been true that the state and the government worked for the benefit of the ruling classes, but it is certain that nowadays neither can continue to exist for such a purpose. It is the responsibility of the politician to think first and foremost of the benefit to the people, but if this leads to the adoption of vote-buying policies designed merely to curry public favour, a resulting bankruptcy of state finances will be inevitable. For a politician who really loves his country and really cares about the welfare of its citizens, surely the most important goal is the creation of a proper balance between healthy financial management and a sound welfare system. Fortunately, one can say that Japanese bureaucrats are very capable and also relatively free from corruption. Since it is up to their good judgement how tax money is spent, one can perhaps say that there is due cause for optimism.

YONEYAMA-Toshinao

Hotels and Inns

In Japan "Western-style" hotels exist alongside *ryokan*, or Japanese inns. It seems useful for visitors from abroad to be aware of the differences between the two.

Western-style hotels also contain Japanese-style rooms, but generally they consist of private rooms with lockable doors and fees are charged by the night. Meals are consumed in the hotel restaurant and alcohol can be drunk at the hotel bar, all services for which one is billed separately. It is also possible to eat and drink in one's room by making use of room service, and services such as dry cleaning are also available, but again separate charges are made. Accommodation is generally charged per person per night and there is a stipulated checking-out time in the morning. The idea of bed-and-breakfast as a package is not one that has become popular in Japan.

In contrast to this, Japanese inns may contain some articles of Western-style furniture, but the rooms do not normally come with a key. From the time when the guest is escorted to the room and served with tea and sweets, the room is complete with a private maid, who leads the guest to the bath, serves dinner, and performs all other necessary services, including laying out the bedding. The bathing facilities are not usually private, regardless of whether or not the inn is located at a hot spring resort. Meals are served in the room. It is possible to have one's underclothes and socks laundered and ironed, and one can move about the inn clad in nightclothes and a robe provided by the inn. Since there is little privacy, valuables should be kept either at the registration desk or else in a safe kept in the room. Accommodation changes are calculated according to the number of nights, and include two meals and taxes. Meals are ranked in a scale according to price and often bear such names as 'pine', 'bamboo', and 'plum'. Rooms normally consist of a unit containing a living room, a waiting room and a corridor overlooking a garden. Prices are relatively lower when groups such as a whole family stay together. However, a gratuity for the services of the maid should be taken into consideration, and there is very little privacy. In this respect, Japanese inns differ from hotels where there is a distinction between the public spaces such as the restaurant and lobby and the private spaces of the rooms for the individual guests. One can say that the functional, contractual Western-style hotels constitute a gesellschaft, while the Japanese inns with their traditions and their family service constitute a gemeinschaft, and that the two exist alongside each other.

Western hotels are of course an import from the West introduced in the 1860s when Japan was opened up to Western countries. The first such hotel is said to have been one that was opened in Yokohama in 1863 by an Englishman. In 1867, the year before the Meiji Restoration, there was also a three-storied hotel with one hundred rooms opened in Tsukiji, in Tokyo. Then in 1878 one was built in Hakone, and in 1890 the Imperial Hotel was opened in Tokyo. The Imperial Hotel later became famous on account of its architecture, which was designed by Frank Lloyd Wright.

Such hotels as these were built principally for the convenience of visiting foreigners and they spread throughout the Tokyo-Yokohama area, the

Kyoto-Osaka-Kobe area and other tourist areas. The Japan Hotel Association was formed in 1941, but even in 1975 it had only 136 members. Hotels were subsequently built all over Japan, and in 1983 there were 349 in all in most parts of the country.

When the numbers of hotels and Japanese inns are added up, they total some eighty thousand, but this is still by no means a large number. Recently cheap and economical business hotels have proved popular with people travelling on business and they are growing in number. Probably the numbers of travellers who prefer to avoid the human contact that inevitably comes with staying in Japanese inns are also on the increase.

Japanese inns have a number of different traditions - there were the inns for daimyo travelling to and from Edo to fulfil their residential obligations there, inns for merchants travelling the country with their wares, inns and lodging houses for pilgrims visiting temples and shrines, and hot-spring inns for those taking the waters. In the Edo period a system of arterial roads developed along with a post-town system offering accommodation along the way, and public peace was well maintained, so the number of travellers grew, some going on pilgrimages to the Ise Shrine, others going to Kyoto to see the sights. The result was that the post-towns became busy and prosperous. In the post-towns along the fifty-three stages of the Tokaido there were as many as 111 inns for the daimyo. On their regular processions to and from Edo the daimyo were accompanied by from sixty to as many as four hundred and fifty attendants, retainers and so on. The tradition of group travel also seen in pilgrimages to Ise has survived to this day in the form of school educational trips and the package tours offered by travel operators.

Oliver Statler's work, *Japanese Inn* (1961), traces the history over four hundred years of a certain inn situated at Okitsu on the Tokaido. He sketches several personalities who later appear in the novel *Shogun* and his story even includes mention of a post-war imperial visit by the Emperor and Empress. In the United States this work was a best-seller.

Even in a 'good old' Japanese inn like this, though, problems have arisen on account of the difficulty of keeping good-quality maids and the rise in labour costs. The old system may very well now be found preserved only at tourist resorts and health spas.

Japanese inns were also generally restaurants. As at the inn in Kawabata Yasunari's *Snow Country*, it was also possible to summon geisha as well. These aspects of the Japanese inn have something in common with the emphasis in hotels on meetings and receptions at which food and drinks are served, such as weddings.

In closing, it should be mentioned that in recent years competition for both Western-style hotels and Japanese inns has been coming from several directions. It takes the form of lodgings run by mutual benefit associations, pensions run by families, hotels for businessmen, and the so-called lovers' hotels at which a room may be rented by the hour.

YONEYAMA-Toshinao

Sex

The ancient myths of Japan are full of episodes concerning sex, sexuality, and reproduction, and of these the best known is that of the creation of the country through the sexual union of a god and a goddess. The first half of the historical chronicle *Kojiki*, which was compiled in 712 AD, consists of a collection of such myths, albeit not a very large one, which contains some thirty-five direct references to sex, including references to sexual intercourse and the sexual organs.

In the literary products of ancient Japan, such as these myths and ballads, there is no trace of any disapproval of expressions relating to sex. On the contrary, they abound with direct references to sexual activity, their metaphors are simple, and they make little use of symbolism. This openness about sex in written materials continued right up to the present day, through the collections of tales of mediaeval Japan, the shunpon (pornographic books) and the ninjōbon (sentimental romances) of the Edo period, and finally the films and literary works of today. In Japanese culture there has been no consciousness of original sin in respect of sex as there has been in Christian cultures.

It is clear from the literary and other works of ancient times that polygamous marriages were common and that there was the custom of 'tsumadoi' whereby men visited the houses of the women they loved. Women had both the right and the ability to refuse men who were courting them. Princess Kaguyahime in the tale *Taketori monogatari* (The Tale of the Bamboo-cutter), which was put together around the beginning of the tenth century, thus succeeds in refusing the offers of marriage put to her by five suitors by giving each of them a difficult task to undertake. A form of the custom of 'tsumadoi' survived up until the Edo period among the commoners in the provinces, especially the young men in farming villages, who would visit the homes of their lovers, a custom known as 'yobai', or 'night-crawling'.

Incest taboos on sexual relations between mother and son, father and daughter, and brother and sister have existed in Japan since the earliest times, and marriage between close relatives is prohibited by civil law. But marriage between cousins is perfectly allowable, and there are no prohibitions in Japan, as there are in China and Korea, on marriage between people with the same surname. In comparison with Christian cultures, there has been in Japan little feeling that masturbation is wrong, nor has there been a taboo on homosexual practices. Among both the samurai and the monks there was for a long time a tradition of paederasty, and in the literature of the Edo period the theme of male homosexuality had an important part to play.

Similarly, there has been in Japan no tradition of performing operations on the genitals for religious reasons such as the operation for circumcision that is practiced in many countries. Furthermore, there has been little admiration or worship of virginity or male chastity.

In the samurai society of the Edo period, however, adultery made a samurai liable to severe punishment, and pre-marital sexual experience was severely discouraged. Puritanical notions, based on Confucian ethics, spread during the Edo period among the samurai, who constituted ten per cent of the entire population. After

the Meiji Restoration of 1868 the Christian Puritanism of Europe and America entered Japan and
from then onwards the sexual culture of Japan
became the target for prohibitions and repression.
Thus in the early years of the Meiji period there
were prohibitions on mixed public bathing and on
the sale of pornography, adultery became a crime
in criminal law, and in civil law the concept of the
illegitimate child was introduced. This series of institutional changes made sex out to be something
vulgar, something to be hidden away, and created
an atmosphere where sexual intercourse itself
was held to be bad unless it took place in a recognized relationship, that is, between husband
and wife. Together with the various movements
for the reform of morals, for the abolition of pros-
titution, and for the emancipation of women,
these measures enforced chastity and purity on
women and encouraged the spread of the ideas
that virginity was valuable and masturbation evil.
There were also prohibitions on the custom
whereby sexual education was entrusted to a
group of young men or women. In other words,
the traditions that formed the sexual culture of
Japan were held to be unsuitable for a country
that was seeking to modernize itself, make itself
prosperous, and nurture a strong army, and as a
consequence they became subject to a good deal
of repression.

On the other hand, in constrast with this 'modern puritanism' on the level of the superficial,
'official culture', there remained among the common people the traditional consciousness of sex
that they had always had. Writers such as Nagai
Kafū (1879-1959) and Tanizaki Junichiro (1886-
1965) protested about the official attitudes and
reacted against them, traditonal rituals continued

to be performed, although they did undergo some changes. After the war, the policy of the occupation forces seemed to have put an end to sexual repression, but the sexual self-indulgence of some of the occupation troops prompted a reaction, and the enforcement of coeducation led to some confusion for a while. Institutional changes, such as the adoption of a new constitution, have gradually led to some freedom of expression in matters pertaining to sex, but pornography and photographs of sexual intercourse are still forbidden, and customs officials still apply black ink to the offending parts of illustrations in foreign magazines.

Japanese values now cover a wide range and so do ways of thinking about sex. Even now, the form of arranged marriage known as the 'miai' marriage is far from dying out, people still use the expression 'marriageable age', and in fact most Japanese experience married life at some time or other. But at the same time there are women who declare themselves to be unmarried mothers, and the divorce rate, although very low by the standards of many foreign countries, is on the increase. It is easy to have a pregnancy terminated by abortion, but there is a boom in 'mizuko jizo', small Buddhist statues commemorating aborted foetuses. And sexual relations are becoming freer, irrespective of whether the partners are married or not. It is reasonable to say that Japan, having passed through a stage of 'modern puritanism', is still in some confusion over sexual matters.

YONEYAMA-Toshinao

]An Ageing Society

In October 1982 the population of Japan was 118,690,000, and is estimated to be increasing by about 810,000 per year. However, this means that the rate of population increase is only 0.69 per cent a year, which is the lowest rate since the war. It is not such a low rate as that of France at 0.4 per cent or the European Economic Community as a whole at 0.2 per cent, but it is lower than the rates of the United States and Canada (both 1.0 per cent), the People's Republic of China (1.4 per cent) and the Soviet Union (0.8 per cent).

The composition of the population of Japan has in recent years started to go through some great changes, and it is thought that the tendencies these reflect are likely to last for some while yet. The principal changes are the reduced number of children aged less than four years and the increased number of people aged sixty-five or over. The population profile is therefore changing from a pyramid shape to a shape closer to that of a jar with narrow base, and it is expected to make further changes in the future so that it ends up lookinglike a beer-barrel. Those aged sixty-five or over now represent 9.6 per cent of the total population, and government offices anticipate that it will reach 15.6 per cent by the year 2000. This means that while at present one in every eleven people is aged sixty-five or more, by 2000 it will be one in every 6.4 people. Of course in Europe and the United States the proportion of old people in the population is in excess of ten per cent and in Sweden and West Germany it is over 15 per cent, so Japan is now approaching the level of those countries. But for more than a century now the old have represented between five and seven per cent of the population of Japan, and if that figure is now approaching that of Europe and America, it is Japan's first experience of such an ageing process.

The population profile of any country shows clearly some of its cultural traditions and historical experiences, and Japan is no exception. Thus the reason there were fewer childern born in 1966 than in normal years was because that year was a special year in the Chinese calendar. In the Chinese cyclical calendar each year is indicated by one of twelve 'branches' and by one of ten 'roots': 1966 was 'hinoeuma', the year of the horse and lesser fire, a combination thought to be particularly unlucky. The cyclical cycle repeats itself every sixty years, so a 'hinoeuma' year comes round only once in that period. Since the middle of the Edo period it has been believed that girls born in this year would have violent disposition and would kill and devour their husbands, and so out of anxiety for the future of their children parents sought to avoid having children in such years. Thus in 1906, too, there was a similar drop in the birth rate.

The children born during the post-war babyboom of 1947-49 have now reached the age of 33-35. That generation was unusually large and in its progress through kindergarten, elementary school, middle school and high school it left behind huge classrooms and created fierce competition for entrance to universities and later for employment. It was also this generation that was at the centre of the university disturbances of the sixties and seventies and provided the activists that took part in the radical Japanese Red Army. In 1971-74, this generation began to produce its own children, which gave rise to a second baby-boom. But the post-war baby-boom was not simply caused by a rise in the birth rate, for owing to the widespread use of antibiotics and other medicines the infant mortality rate declined, too, allowing many more children to survive than would have done before.

At present the average number of children per family in Japan is 2.2, a level that is one of the lowest in the world. It is thanks to the advances of medicine and a medical insurance system that this trend towards a small number of births and low infant mortality has arisen.

As the birth rate has changed, so too has the environment surrounding the raising of children. Most births now take place in maternity clinics, and each mother receives a notebook in which to record the details of her child's health. The health insurance office thus plays a part in caring for the health of the child. Mothers expend a lot of energy on the raising and education of their children, but it has also been pointed out that health or personality problems can arise in children depending on the manner of child-rearing. Such problems as a dislike of milk, asthma, habitual stomach pains, chronic diarrhoea, late development of the ability to talk, truancy, violence towards parents in the home and so on are put down to mothers with poor child-raising skills or to fathers who have little to do with the raising of their own children. Problems concerning children, including truancy and violence at school, are receiving constant attention in the news programmes these days. Babies have been abandoned in coin-lockers or on rubbish heaps, while education-mad mothers send their children to cramming schools after regular school hours, and children who cannot keep up in school any more drop out and form their own subcultures such as that of the leather-jacketed boys who race up and down the roads at night on motorbikes.

On the other hand, the life expectancy for Japanese in 1981 had risen to 73.79 for men and 79.13 for women. This is the highest figure for men in the world, while for women it is the second highest, after Iceland. These figures change every year, but it is a fact that the Japanese enjoy a high life expectancy. As of September 1982 there were exactly one thousand two hundred people over hundred years old in Japan. That number has been on the increase over the last eleven years and is constantly setting new records in Japan. According to the Guinness Books of Records, the oldest person in the world for whom reliable evidence can be found is Mr Shigechiyo Izumi, who lives on one of the islands in Kagoshima Prefecture and was born in 1865.

A number of elderly people are active and wield a lot of influence in financial, educational and other circles, but there are also old people who are confined to their beds and live alone. Respect for the aged and family ties provide support for the elderly in society, and social welfare facilities for them are also well established, including pensions, medical care, and free passes for transportation. The main problem now is how the burden of providing for the aged in society is going to be met in the future.

YONEYAMA-Toshinao

Rapid Economic Growth in the 60s

The 1960's witnessed a unique phenomenon in the history of Japan, one which is of special importance to the Japanese people and perhaps to the whole world.

In economic terms, this era was marked by an astonishing growth in the country's GNP (Gross National Product), which expanded at an annual rate of over 10% over a period of ten years. It is for this reason that the name "Era of Rapid Economic Growth" was coined.

Towards the end of 1960, the Cabinet of Prime Minister Hayato Ikeda published a policy paper entitled "Plan for the Doubling of the People's Income", which aimed at doubling the average per capita income of the Japanese over a ten-year period. In actual fact this goal was attained even faster than planned, within a mere seven years. If one were to express real per capita income in 1960 as 100 units, then in 1970 this had risen to 245, and by 1973 had reached a level of 301. This is what is meant by the phrase "rapid economic growth".

The beginnings of this upheaval can be traced back to 1956, the year in which it was officially stated that the country had emerged from the "postwar period". Prime Minister Ikeda's plan was set on firm foundations. Already in the years 1953 to 1955 per capita income had grown in real terms at an annual rate of 8.1%, increasing yet further to 8.6% in the next four years, 1956 to 1960. The doubling plan was a policy decision based on the trend of the times.

The Tokyo Olympic Games, held in October of 1964, were a national spectacle that highlighted the first half of this era of rapid growth. In contrast, the International Exposition which took place in Osaka over a six-month period from March to September of 1970 served as symbolic climax to the latter half of the era. The first oil crisis of 1973 dealt a heavy blow to the economy, and Japan even experienced a period of negative growth in the GNP. This marked a switch from the rapid growth to a new era of low growth.

The Olympic Games and the International Exposition - held in the largest cities of east and west Japan respectively - were both extremely successful events.

The Tokyo Olympics had originally been planned back in 1940, but the Pacific War forced cancellation. The first Olympic Games ever staged in Asia was achieved 24 years later. Three thousand atheletes from 94 countries participated in a total of 20 different events; after 30 years the long-cherished desire of Japan's amateur sportsmen and fans had been granted. The opening ceremony with the emperor's address, various memorable highlights, and the happy spectacle of the closing ceremony, all were relayed on television and are still fondly remembered, the subject of many a nostalgic chat.

The Osaka International Exposition - known better as "Expo'70" - was held over a six-month period on the Senri hills of Suita City, just north of Osaka. The theme of Expo '70 was "Human Progress and Harmony" and it attracted some 64,220,000 visitors to the pavilions of the 77 participating countries. It has been calculated that over 60% of the Japanese population saw Expo '70.

With these national events in mind, the municipal authorities of both Tokyo and Osaka launched large-scale projects for the enhancement of the urban environment. Especial attention was paid to improving city transit systems with the hurried construction of subways and expressways. Of course, these still exist, as do the various Olympic facilities - such as the stadium and the athletes' village - which have remained as permanent installations and are still used. The site of Expo '70 has similarly been turned into a memorial park, complete with a new Museum of Ethnology and Modern Art Gallery.

It was in the year of the Tokyo Olympics that the famous Bullet Train first became operational, running between Tokyo and Osaka. Also, the Meishin (Nagoya - Kobe) and Tōmei (Tokyo - Nagoya) highways were completed in the year before Expo '70. These two events thus had far-reaching consequences, not just to the cities which were directly involved, but also to the transportation network of the whole country.

The expressways built in connection with the Games and the Exposition certainly changed the appearance of the city centres. For instance, Nihonbashi in downtown Tokyo, which used to be called the hub of the country's road network, is now overshadowed by an overhead expressway which straddles the once-famous landmark. Similarly, the riverside view that could be enjoyed around Osaka's Naka-no-shima has been completely altered by the roads which now monopolize the area. But the road network which was formed by these expressways has itself given the cities brand-new urban vistas. The roads, together with the expanded subway network, have greatly changed the transit patterns in Japan's big cities, thus altering the travelling habits of its inhabitants.

Rapid economic growth also accelerated the pace of change in the life styles of the Japanese people to a considerable extent. For example, the "three sacred treasures" of the average household in Japan - the washing machine, the refrigerator and the television - were forced to relinquish their honored position to a new trio: the car, the air conditioner and the colour television. These new "treasures" spread rapidly throughout the country. Other large consumer durables, such as pianos and western-style beds, also became commonplace items in people's lives. These changes in the types of personal belongings of the Japanese represented a sudden boost in material wealth. Supermarkets sprung up as a result of the great improvement in goods distribution. Instant foods appeared on the shelves. And there was an explosive growth in the mass leisure industry, with skiing and tourist travel becoming popular pastimes.

These changes in people's life styles directly encouraged migration into the urban centres, unfortunately leading to the problems of overcrowding on the one hand, and depopulation on the other. Rapid growth also brought with it the threat of pollution and pollution-related health problems. Various other negative effects, dubbed the "backlash of rapid economic growth", remain even now as a legacy of the era. Nevertheless, despite the losses and problems engendered by this "revolution", the material gains and qualitative improvement enjoyed by Japanese society as a whole are surely beyond dispute.

YONEYAMA-Toshinao

New Town

One of the greatest changes in Japan since the Second World War has been the rapid progress of urbanization throughout the country. Roughly speaking, before the war seven people out of ten were living in farming villages and leading a traditional kind of life. But in the twenty-five years following the end of the war the numbers of people whose lives mainly depended on agriculture underwent a dramatic decline, and the situation is now reversed so that 718 people in every thousand are pursuing urban life-styles.

This has meant that areas of agricultural land have increasingly been taken over by housing developers as the towns and cities expanded and have turned into suburban residential areas. Once a tract of land has been allocated to the construction of urban dwellings, an infrastructure of electrical, water and gas supplies and road access is provided, and the housing itself often consists of high-rise apartment buildings constructed by companies with large amounts of investment capital to draw upon. These are the 'new towns', the 'housing complexes' (jūtaku danchi). One example is the new town which developed in the Senri hills to the north of Osaka: from 1961 onwards on a site there covering 1160 square kilometres, a new town has been built consisting of 37,330 houses and containing a population of some 130,000 people. Once it was clear that this project was proving to be a success, similar kinds of projects were started up all over the country. Under the auspices of the Japan Housing Corporation and the local governments in a number of the prefectures and cities of Japan, a number of such large-scale new towns have now been constructed - amongst them are Tsukuba Gakuen Toshi (2700 square kilometres, 160,000 people) and Tama New Town (3011 square kilometres, 400,000 people) in the Tokyo area, Suma New Town (940 square kilometres, 118,000 people) to the west of Kobe, Chiba New Town (2913 square kilometres, 340,000 people) in Chiba Prefecture, and Senboku New Town (1520 square kilometres, 188,000 people) to the south of Osaka.

In some cases thinking has developed beyond the idea of simply building a suburban residential district and has included the creation of new employment opportunities by moving government research bodies and universities to the new site, as has happened in the case of Tsukuba Gakuen

High-rise apartment complex in Takashimadaira, Tokyo (Kyodo)

Toshi. It seems likely that this trend will continue in the future, as can be seen from the plan to build a similar new town between Nara and Kyoto.

Japan has a long history of urban development which goes back to the planned construction of Heijo-kyo in Nara and of Heian-kyo in Kyoto in the seventh and ninth centuries respectively. In the sixteenth and seventeenth centuries there was the construction of the castle town of Azuchi by Oda Nobunaga and of Fushimi and Osaka by Toyotomi Hideyoshi, followed in the years since the Meiji Restoration (1868) by Kobe, Yokohama and Sapporo. And it is well known that in the middle of the eighteenth century Edo and Osaka had larger populations than the cities of Europe. In modern times, before the war, there have also been a number of attempts to build planned cities, but they cannot all be said to have been particularly successful: the plans developed by Goto Shinpei's 'Tokyo Municipal Government Investigative Committee', which started work in 1922, were not fully realized.

An interesting phenomenon is the role played by the private railway companies in the Kansai area around Osaka and Kyoto in encouraging the development of residential areas along the routes followed by their railways. In the hope of increasing the numbers of their passengers they have even encouraged the construction of baseball grounds and the formation of a girls' operetta troupe to provide entertainment. Thus they have been involved in the construction of suburban residential areas with a modern flavour, and these have developed into model residential areas for the new middle and upper-middle classes. Even in the new towns one finds not only the high-rise apartment blocks which have been referred to as 'rabbit hutches' abroad, and superior apartment complexes, but also areas consisting of detached houses, each with its own garden. Many Japanese aspire to such a detached house with garden as a symbol of their advancement, but since it is difficult to realize these ambitions, the situation is giving rise to some dissatisfaction.

The new towns contain supermakets and department stores and meeting places of all kinds, and there is a lot of lively community activity. It will, however, take some time before the new life-style of the new towns, one that differs both from the traditional rural and modern urban life-styles, develops to maturity. Thus in the 'sprawly' areas where long hours of commuting are required, there is dissatisfaction with the distances to be travelled at night, with the sense of danger, poor road access, poor transportation and shopping facilities, the lack of medical facilities, parks, swimming pools and recreation grounds, and the difficulty of obtaining fresh food. And the formation of new human relations and a new sense of community to take the place of traditional rural cooperative communities or neighbourhood communities in the towns is not proving easy. Kindergarten and elementary school PTAs can contribute to a sense of community, and cooperative societies and radical citizens' protest groups may develop.

But the life-style of industrial or post-industrial society is spreading thanks to television and the mass media and is gradually becoming the norm among the Japanese people. After all it is already twenty years since the first people moved into Senri New Town north of Osaka, and the 'new town babies' are now on the verge of adulthood.

YONEYAMA-Toshinao

¦The Information Society

Apart from body language, such as gestures, the oldest means of communication is by word of mouth. In nonliterate cultures, oral traditions developed: these are still widely present in the form of gossip or word-of-mouth communication in a small group. Japan, however, has a long tradition of using ideogrammatic characters. The ancient oral traditions were written down in the *Kojiki* (records of ancient matters), *Nihon-shoki* (chronicles of Japan) and *Manyoshu* (anthology of Japanese poems). In Japan, communication has been in literate form since at least the seventh century. Independently of literature, whether poetry or historical documents, all documents issued by the Imperial Court were symbolic of its authority. All ranks and bureaucratic positions, including 'Kampaku' (the principal advisor to the Emperor) and 'Shogun' (generalissimo of the Emperor's army) were verified in writing. The documents issued by the Emperors, ex-Emperors in religious orders and shoguns were instruments of its authority, occasionally being a source of dispute. After the 13th century, the land certificates issued by the registry office were guaranteed as vested rights even after a man of power was replaced. 'Notes of guarantee', granted by the man who unified the nation, to his subordinate district lords, were, in other words, the guarantee of the district authority invested by the central authority. The central authority himself had to receive from the court the title of Kampaku or Shogun. Japan has long rested on a political structure in which virtual power was backed up by nominal authority. Such structure was in turn supported by 'information' in written form.

Information was communicated orally or by ideograms via messengers. Gongs, drums and trumpet shells also conveyed some messages.

In the 17th century, with the development of transportation networks, express messengers were employed to convey urgent messages. In urban areas, 'Kawaraban' or 'Yomiuri', single-sheet block printed newspapers, were issued on an irregular basis. However, the development of a full-scale communication network began with the postal service, which was inaugurated as a national enterprise in the Meiji Era. Later, the telegraph and telephone were developed gradually. After World War Ⅱ, telephones spread rapidly, making Japan the second largest telephone-using nation, following the U.S.. The scope of communication will be further expanded by launching communication satellites.

In the age of chronic civil strife (mid-fifteenth century), the collection and use of information were of equal importance to military power. Those who were aware of its importance grew in power, expanded their influence, and ultimately took leadership. The unification of Japan by Nobunaga, Hideyoshi and Ieyasu was the result of espionage activities, as well as military power: the value of information was highly emphasized.

A pharmaceutical company gathers prominent researchers in its laboratory and spends a lot of money and time in developing new medicines. Such medicine is a valuable property; But the property is not the medicine itself, but the know-how information as to its components and manufacturing process. Leakage of information to a competitor is known as industrial espionage, which occasionally occurs today, generating much publicity. Noteworthy was an international industrial espionage case which occurred recently. As the value of information comes to be widely accepted, the rights to protect information, such as patents and copyrights, are being regulated. On the other hand, there is a movement to deny exclusive use of such information, to make them available to the public.

Information is communicated by voice, characters, figures, tables, photos, pictures, video and many other means. The communication media range from human voice and letters to huge international communications systems. The media equipment, facilities and systems, such as radios, televisions, telephones and tape recorders, have developed into rapidly growing industrial fields. In response to the development and spread of computers, the development of even more advanced communication systems is expected. Information today plays a critical role in the media system, that is, the hardware and manufacturing industries.

But more important is software—the information itself. In today's information-oriented society, information is becoming increasingly important. With such weight given to the information industry, Japan has been taking a leading role in hardware, such as electrical appliances and cameras. In terms of software production, namely information, Japan has often been on the information receiving side, with fewer occasions of providing information. However in the future, Japan should be on the providing side as one of Asia's advanced nations, and will act as a global information centre, along with Europe and North America.

UMESAO-Tadao

Chronology of Japan and World Events

Japan	World
BC8000:Jōmon period.	
3000:Shell mounds.	BC3000:Emergence of civilization at the Indus River valley and the Yellow River valley.
400:Yayoi period. Use of bronze and iron. Irrigated rice cultivation.	221:Unification of China by Shi Hwan.
	27:Founding of Roman Empire.
AD 239:Queen Himiko of the country of Yamatai sent mission to China.	AD 395:Division of the Empire; Arcadius emperor in East, Honorius in West.
	486:Founding of Frank Kingdom.
593:Regency of Prince Shotoku; Seventeen Article Constitution promulgated. Establishment of Horyuji Temple, the oldest wooden architecture. Dispatch of Japanese embassies to China.	589:Sui Dynasty in China.
	610:Founding of Islam by Muhammad.
	618:End of Sui Dynasty; Tang Dynasty began in China.
	624:Tang Dynasty; Establishment of centralized bureaucracy, Law and Code institution, taxation and farmland allotment rule.
	642:Fading of Sassanid Dynasty in Persia.
645:Taika coup d'etat, followed by Reform; Initiation of law and code institution. Census registration. Farmland allotment rule.	
701:Taiho law Code. Founding of the higher educational system, and Tenpyo culture flourished.	
708:First issuance of copper coinage.	
710:Founding of Heijo capital(Nara).	
712:Compilation of the oldest histories: "Kojiki" and "Nihon-shoki".	
752:Dedication of the Great Buddha of Todaiji Temple in Nara.	
771:Compilation of the oldest anthology "Man'yoshu".	
794:Founding of Heian capital(Kyoto).	800:Leo crowned Charlemagne Emperor of the West.
894:Dispatch of the last embassy to China; Development of Japanese culture. Invention of kana phonetic syllabary; "Taketori monogatari"(Tale of the Bamboo Cutter), "Ise monogatari" (Tales of Ise), etc. Waka poetry flourished; "Kokinshu" and other anthologies edited.	

Japan	World
	907:End of Tang Dynasty
	962:Otto I, King of Germany, crowned Emperor by John XII.
	983:Capet Dynasty in France.
1000:Female literature flourished: Writing of "Genji Monogatari" (Tale of Genji) by Lady Murasaki Shikibu, and "Makura no Soshi"(Pillow Book) by Lady Sei Shonagon.	1054:Schism of Greek and Roman Catholic.
	1096:The People's Crusade.
	1206:Unification of Mongolia by Genghis Khan.
1192:Assumption of the title of shogun by Yoritomo. Founding of shogunal government at Kamakura.	1215:Enactment of Magna Carta in England.
1224:Founding of Zen sect and Jodo sect.	
1232:Issuance of the Joei Shikimoku (Kamakura law code), Japan's first samurai family rule.	1241:Establishment of the Hanseatic League.
1274:First Mongol invasion. Development of military crafts(armor swords, etc.).	1271:Trip to the East by Marco Polo.
	1300:Renaissance.
1338:Transfer of shogunal government to Kyoto by Ashikaga(Ashikaga period).	1338:Outbreak of the Hundred Year's War between England and France.
	1429:Joan of Arc raised the seige of Orleans. Invention of movable type by Gutenberg.
1467:Onin War; With the government power weakened, civil wars broke out, bringing the warring states period. Sakai developed autonomy.	1455:Outbreak of the War of the Roses in England.
	1494:Columbus discovered America.
	1519:Magellan began circulation of globe. Protestant Reformation led by Luther.
1543:Arrival of the Portuguese at Tanegashima; introduction of firearms.	1543:Copernicus set forth the Copernican theory.
1549:Arrival of St.Francis Xavier in Kyushu; the start of the Christian missionary movement.	
	1571:Spain conquered the Philippines.
1573:End of the Ashikaga shogunate.	
1576:Transfer of Nobunaga to Azuchi castle on the Lake Biwa.	
1590:Hideyoshi supreme in Japan.	
1600:Victory of Ieyasu at the Battle of Sekigahara.	1600:England established the British East India Company.
1603:Assumption of the title of shogun by Ieyasu. Founding of shogunal government at Edo(Tokyo).	1602:Holland established the Dutch East India Company.
1604:Shuin-jo(red official seal) issued by shogun to trading ships. Mileposts provided along five Highways for road development.	1604:France established the French East India Company.
1609:Establishment of the Dutch trading post at Hirado.	

Japan	World
	1613:Romanov Dynasty in Russia.
1620:Establishment of Japanese towns at Siam and Luzon.	
1635:Sakoku-rei(seclusion order) promulgated; ban on Japanese travel abroad and return home.	
1637:Shimabara rebellion(suppression of Christianity).	1642:The Puritan Revolution in England.
1643:Institutional foundation of the Tokugawa shogunate completed; perpetual ban on farmland trade.	
Expansion of Terakoya(school system operated by Buddhist temples) from cities to towns.	1660:The Restoration of Royal Rule in England.
Development of commercial capital.	1661:Personal government of Louis XIV.
1668:Start of Genroku Era; ukiyo-e(genre painting and block prints) kabuki drama, novels and haiku(17-syllable poem in the five-seven-five pattern) flourished.	
1722:Promotion of development of new farmlands.	1767:Invention of steam engine by Watt.
1774:Dutch studies flourished; Translation of "Tafel Anatomia " under the title of Kaitai Shinsho.	1770:Industrial Revolution in England.
	1775:Outbreak of the War of Independence in the United States.
Development of factory-style establishments, such as for silk reeling, fabric and brewing.	1789:Outbreak of the French Revolution.
1853:Arrival of Commandore Mattew C. Perry at Uraga.	
1854:Treaty of Kanagawa with the United States.	
1868:Meiji Restoration.	1869:Outbreak of the Opium War.
1871:Return of daimyo domains to the Emperor.	1869:Opening of the Suez Canal.
Promotion of industrial protection and development.	
1872:Opening of telegraph between Tokyo and Osaka.	
Opening of the railway between Tokyo and Yokohama.	
1873:Inauguration of universal military service.	
1878:Opening of telephones between Tokyo and Osaka.	1878:Invention of electric light by Edison.
First use of arc lamp.	
1884:Progress of modern mechanical industry.	
1888:Establishment of city assemblies and the reorganization of the local governments.	

Japan	World
1889:Promulgation of the Constitution and the Imperial House Act. Opening of Tokaido line. 1890:First general election for Diet. First session of Imperial Diet assembly. 1892:Extension of hydraulic power industry. First industrial revolution(light industry). 1894:Sino-Japanese War. Strike at a cotton mill in Osaka. 1895:Invention of power loom by Sakichi Toyota. 1896:Imports of motion pictures. Start of domestic film production. 1904:Russo-Japanese War. Development of radio communications. Second industrial revolution(heavy industry). Development of shipbuilding engineering.	 1897:Invention of radio communication. 1903:First manned flight by Wright brothers. 1905:China Revolution led by YAT-SEN.
1910:Annexation of Korea. 1912:First participation in the International Olympic Games. Spread of democracy. 1920:Japan admitted into the League of Nations. 1923:Great Kanto earthquake. 1925:Declaration of General Election Law. Start of radio broadcasting. 1937:Outbreak of war with China. 1941:Outbreak of the Pacific War. 1945:Atomic bombing of Hiroshima and Nagasaki. The end of the war. 1946:Declaration of the Constitution of Japan. Second agricultural reform. 1951:Peace Conference in San Francisco. 1953:Start of television broadcasting. 1956:Japan admitted into the United Nations. 1964:Tokyo Olympic Games. Opening of the Shinkansen(bullet train) between Tokyo and Osaka. 1970:Opening of the World Exposition in Osaka. Launch of the domestic satellite. 1975:The Shinkansen extended to Fukuoka.	 1917:Outbreak of the Russian Revolution. 1931:Outbreak of the Manchurian Incident. 1939:German invasion of Poland. Outbreak of the Pacific War. 1946:Independence of Indonesia. 1950:Outbreak of the Korean War. 1957:First space satellite — the Russian "Sputnik". 1960:African nations gained independence from France. 1967:Outbreak of the Middle East War. 1969:First lunar landing by U.S. "Appolo 11" 1972:England admitted to EC. 1975:End of the Vietnam War.